Soccer Techniques, Tactics & Teamwork

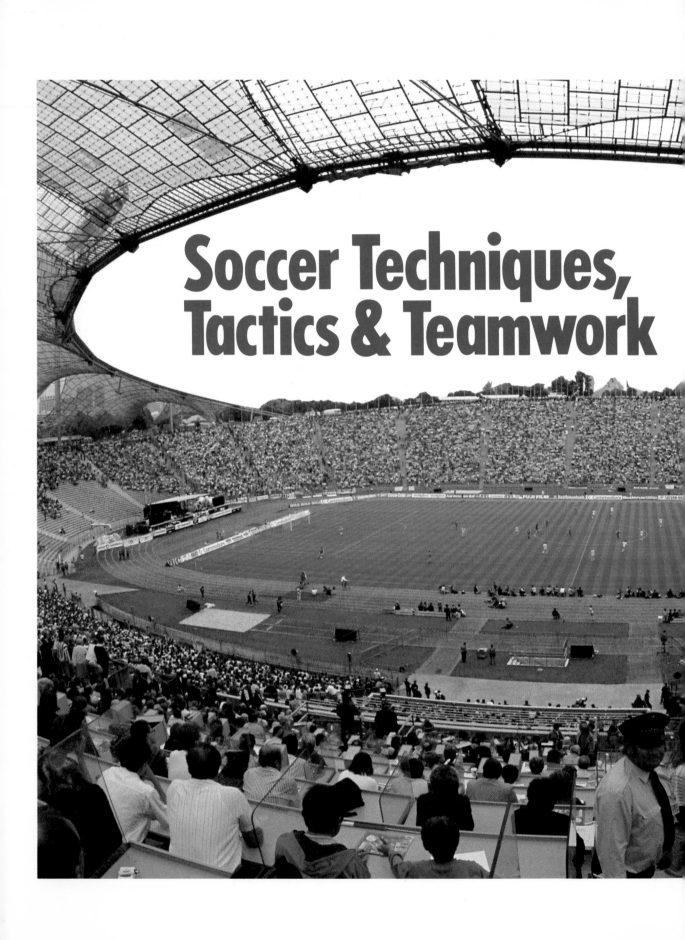

Soccer Techniques, Tactics & Teamwork

Gerhard Bauer

Introduction by Franz Beckenbauer

Sterling Publishing Co., Inc.   New York

Demonstration of Techniques:

Markus Ebner

Max Echschlager

Stefan Heigenhauser

Dean Spanring

Ernst Thaler

Photo Credits:

Adidas:	148, 149
Bauer:	108
Baumann:	92
Birkner:	8, 38, 39, 40, 45, 48, 49, 52, 53, 54, 56, 57, 64, 67, 69, 79, 80, 81, 116, 144, 146, 147
Bongarts:	96
Erhard, GmbH:	146, 147, 150
Kemmler:	42/43, 46, 47, 50/51, 52/53, 54/55, 99
Mühlberger:	2/3, 7, 10, 18, 27/26, 36, 72, 77, 84, 93, 121, 123, 129, 132
Sinicki:	59, 61, 88, 111
Winkler:	140

Front Cover Photo: Baumann

Translated by Elisabeth E. Reinersmann

Library of Congress Cataloging-in-Publication Data

Bauer, Gerhard, 1940-
    [Lehrbuch Fussball.   English]
    Soccer techniques, tactics, & teamwork / Gerhard Bauer ;
  introduction by Franz Beckenbauer.
       p. cm.
    Translation of: Lehrbuch Fussball.
    Includes index.
    ISBN 0-8069-8730-8
    1. Soccer—Training. 2. Soccer—Coaching. I. Title. II. Title:
  Soccer techniques, tactics, and teamwork.
  GV943.9.T7B3813 1993
  796.344'07—dc20   92-44087
                                                  CIP

10 9 8 7 6 5 4 3 2 1

Published 1993 by Sterling Publishing Company, Inc.
387 Park Avenue South, New York, N.Y. 10016
Originally published by BLV Verlagsgesellschaft mbH
under the title *Lehrbuch Fußball*
© 1990 by Verlagsgesellschaft mbH, München
English translation © 1993 by Sterling Publishing Inc.
Distributed in Canada by Sterling Publishing
℅ Canadian Manda Group, P.O. Box 920, Station U
Toronto, Ontario, Canada M8Z 5P9
Distributed in Great Britain and Europe by Cassell PLC
Villiers House, 41/47 Strand, London WC2N 5JE, England
Distributed in Australia by Capricorn Link Ltd.
P.O. Box 665, Lane Cove, NSW 2066
Printed and bound in Hong Kong
All rights reserved

Sterling ISBN 0-8069-8730-8

Contents

Contents

Soccer, a game that continues to fascinate its fans, is considered the number-one sport in the world. Recently, I was reminded of this fact when I looked at the statistical data: Every four years, 15 billion viewers watch the World Championship Games, a number that is difficult to comprehend.

As a fan and a representative of this sport, I could look at these numbers, and lean back, satisfied and relaxed, basking in the glow of being in first place. But this would be the beginning of the end, because sitting still is the equivalent of sliding back. This is particularly true in the game of soccer.

I applaud the publication of a new book on soccer. I think it is justified, since new developments in this game are taking place all the time.

I also think that those who often say that soccer was much better in the past are wrong and unfair. I suggest that those who feel this way buy a video of the 1970 World Championship Games in Mexico. If they watch the semifinals, which Germany lost to Italy by a score of three to four, they will understand that it is the drama and excitement that keeps soccer alive.

People will most likely notice something else. In those days, players had much more time. Although the old motto "Stop—look—play" isn't necessarily observed anymore, they moved a little faster than that. But I would still insist that any national championship team today had better play a lot faster. Modern players are not only under time pressure, they are under constant pressure even in open spaces. Thus, occasional technical mistakes can't be avoided.

It is wrong, however (and this brings me back to the point I tried to make in the beginning), to believe that the technical skills of the players were much better in the past. This is also true of the tactical skills. Modern soccer is asking much more of players today.

I have noticed that corner and free kicks are not used nearly as often as they should be. Why that is so I couldn't say. This observation, which my colleague Hannes Löhr also voiced recently, is surely another reason why the publication of a soccer book, outlining the process of training and teaching, is very timely. This book attempts to inspire and to give new impetus to daily training sessions with the goal of improving technical and tactical skills as well as increasing fitness.

Have fun with Gerhard Bauer's book.

Franz Beckenbauer

Introduction

Soccer, now and in the past, is one of the most attractive types of sports. This is true not only of the active player, but also for the fan who comes to the stadium or watches on TV.

There are huge numbers of un-officially organized teams and players that meet on a more-or-less regular basis in their free time for the sheer pleasure of playing the game. Also, as surveys of students have shown, soccer is a favorite in school athletic programs.

In spite of this, we must not forget that the competition never goes to sleep. In my capacity as head of the Association of German Soccer Teachers, I have the chance to speak with coaches from all sectors of soccer. The one topic discussed most often is the problem of attracting new talent. In part, this is due to the competition soccer faces from other sports, the changes in the way children spend their free time, and the decline of street soccer. Consequently, it is very difficult to find young people with natural talent. Coaches are truly worried. But keep in mind that problems are here to be solved. Those who are responsible, including the coaches, must look for new and innovative ideas to remedy this situation. Besides intensifying their search for talent and concentrating on appropriate but passionate leadership, the actual training must take into consideration all that we have learned from practical experience and from research in sports medicine. From the very start, young players should receive age-appropriate training in accordance with the criteria outlined herein. Exercise programs should be designed to strengthen competitiveness. Only then can we hope to stand up to the challenges of the future.

Everybody involved in the nurturing and training of players and teams (including the players themselves) will find the information and knowledge necessary for a successful training program—for young people as well as for adults—in this book. I have included all that I have learned during my many years as a coach in amateur and college soccer and the knowledge I have gained as a college phys ed teacher (with emphasis on soccer). I hope it will be helpful to coaches and players of all levels.

I would be very happy, dear reader, if this book increases your enjoyment of the sport, and if it makes the work of coaches a little easier.

Gerhard Bauer

Gerhard Bauer

Attractions of the Game

The game of soccer, which has captivated people over the centuries, is still gaining in popularity all over the world. Its attraction has many different roots. What is it that makes soccer so fascinating to players and fans alike?

The Attraction for Players

Soccer and the Need for Physical Activity

Small children, kicking and running after a ball, are following their innate desire for moving, leaping, running, and jumping, all vital for healthy development.

The joy of playing with a ball grows in direct proportion to the increase in the skills. Players of all ages get great satisfaction from being able to move a ball with their feet or their head. The ability to dribble expertly or to aim a kick accurately is a source of joy.

The Hunting Instinct and Soccer

Humans have survived over many centuries by hunting. The hunting and fighting instincts are deeply rooted in our psyche. As civilization has made gains, it has also greatly limited the possibility for men to exercise this basic instinct. Sports, particularly ball sports such as soccer, offer a means to satisfy this innate need. The "hunt" after the ball, the confrontation and competition between players, the successful mastery of dangerous moments during the game, the roar of applause after successfully kicking a goal, for the modern player these satisfy some of the same instincts

that must have guided the successful hunter in the distant past.

Soccer and the Impulse to Play

The sport of soccer has all the elements and characteristics of a game—at least for young people and amateurs. It is an activity undertaken freely. It is goal specific and limited by rules and by a clearly defined space within which to play. It can be repeated time and time again, and the outcome is never quite certain.

No one is forced to play. Concentration on the game allows all the participants to forget everyday concerns. The consequences of a game lost or of points lost can be made up the next time. Losses are never permanent and, therefore, not as painful as "losing" in school or on the job.

The uncertainty or ambivalence about the outcome of the game is the driving force for players and fans alike. Up to the very last second of the game, the proverbial Sword of Damocles hangs over every emotionally packed action. Will possession of the ball, an attempt at passing, a confrontation between two opponents, an attempt at kicking a goal, or any of the other countless possible combinations work out as anticipated— or not?

Fans and players alike are constantly torn between hope and despair. Emotions are charged, only to be relieved moments later. In other words, soccer speaks with great intensity to the play instinct in humans.

Group Participation and Soccer

Human beings are social animals. A player is able to find his place in the hierarchical order of the team.

The star and the utility player complement each other. Fans in the stadium have a nearly perfect means of satisfying their herd instinct, an instinct inherited from the earliest Homo sapiens.

The Attraction for Fans

Soccer as Theatre

The simplicity of the rules allows soccer fans in the stadium to witness all of the technical finesse of the action, the dramatic high points, as well as the frustrations and deep disappointments. In essence, the fans are not only passive observers but participants, critically and mentally involved in the action on the field. In addition, fans with playing experience are able to anticipate developments on the field, comparing the particular strategy they would have used with what is really happening. In contrast to the players on the field, they never physically experience the consequences of *their* strategy.

Furthermore, fans are an essential part of the overall scenario. They become actors, giving their approval or disapproval, waving flags and banners, clapping rhythmically and frantically, whistling and hollering. Their actions make them an integral part of the whole spectacle.

Soccer as Fertile Ground for Hero Worship

You may understand it or only register the fact with slight amusement, you may condemn it or participate, but the game of soccer, and professional soccer in particular, gives rise to considerable hero worship and creates an army of unconditionally loyal worshippers.

Fans are fascinated by their

The Game of Soccer

The game of soccer satisfies many instinctive drives.

hero's accomplishments, cheering him on, often exploding into thunderous applause. They get carried away by the fancy display of expert skills. They admire the star's ability to maneuver the ball, his staying power, and the craftiness and cleverness with which he handles his opponents.

The object of this adulation is celebrated, envied, and worshipped all at the same time. It is a known phenomenon that hero worship thrives in regions that have high unemployment.

Game Characteristics

Like every other game, soccer is

The Basis of the Game

Two teams with 11 players apiece (one of whom is the goalkeeper) play against each other. The winner is the team that, at the end of a set time period, has scored more goals than its opponent. With the exception of the goalkeeper, no player can touch the ball with his hands. Players must kick the ball or hit it with their head or body.

distinguished by a special feature. Its structure is uniquely its own and gives the game its special character. The reason it is so en-

thusiastically played, particularly by young people, is because of the simplicity of its concept: scoring goals, without using your hands. That is the basic, original idea of soccer. This uncomplicated idea makes it possible for the game to be played with the most rudimentary of rules. In addition, soccer can be played in almost any place. A backyard or even a cement surface can become a playing field. Branches placed on the ground at each end of the playing field can be substituted for the goal. Sidelines can be easily marked with backpacks or even sweaters. The same flexibility holds true for the ball. Soccer played for the sheer fun of it does not need a regulation ball; if need be, even a tennis ball will do.

Even for official matches, the rules can be adjusted without losing the original idea of the game. For instance, indoor games have different rules. Teams composed of children under the age of 12 have seven players and play on smaller fields. In addition, the length of the game and the size of the ball can be changed without a problem. Despite these adjustments, the concept of the game remains the same.

Structure of the Game
Every sport has its characteristic structure. Even the games that are similar in concept differ considerably in their structure. Compared to handball, volleyball, and basketball, soccer differs in the following characteristics:

- In soccer, only the goalkeeper may use his hands, and then, only as long as he is in the penalty area.
- In relation to the number of players involved, the playing field is larger than for most other sports. The normal size of a soccer field (see also diagram on page 13) is 345 feet by 230 feet (105 × 70 m). This is approximately 5 times as large as a handball court, 9 times as large as a basketball court, and about 24 times as large as a volleyball court.
- The space in which each player can operate is also larger. Each soccer player has more than 5 times as much space as a handball player and almost 9 times as much space as a basketball player does.
- Fewer goals are scored per game in soccer than most other sports.

Usually the final score is very close, adding to the tension for players and fans alike.
- Confrontations between opposing players happen frequently. An analysis of games has shown that 250 to 350 confrontations between two opposing players take place during a game of professional teams. During matches between France and Germany at the 1982 World Championships, 263 such individual confrontations were counted, and in 1986 there were 309.
- Goal kicking is preceded by a combination of systematic ball maneuvers that includes the use of the midfield, where both teams fight intensely for control of the ball.
- Contact with the ball is unique in soccer. Only in soccer is the ball received and carried with the foot and the head. Aside from soccer, only football and rugby use the foot for kicking goals.
- The amount of time an individual player is in actual possession of the ball is relatively short when measured against the time it takes to play the whole game or the frequency with which a player actually has ball contact. In 1976, Jaschok/Witt timed players' actual ball contact. The study showed the following: Maximum time of contact was 3:50 minutes, minimum was 20 seconds, and the average was about 2 minutes for 50 ball contacts.

Rules of the Game
The FIFA (Fédération Internationale de Football Association) is the international authority that estab-

lishes the rules and governs the sport of soccer. These rules are binding for all international competition between male teams. Games played by children and women and those played indoors (and with some limitations for amateur teams) can be amended by the respective state or local authorities.

The rules that are in effect today have a long and turbulent history. The following is a list of the most important dates in soccer.

1846 A team consists of between 15 and 20 players.
1863 Soccer separates from rugby.
1864 It becomes mandatory to wear shorts that cover the knees and to wear caps with tassels.
1866 The corner kick and free throw are introduced.
1870 The number of players per team is reduced to 11.
1871 The ball may not be stopped with the hands.
1872 Catching the ball with the hands is allowed again, but only for one player. The goalkeeper is born. He may use his hands, but only in the penalty area.
1874 Robert Koch publishes the first book of soccer rules in German. The first German student team is founded in Braunschweig.
1875 The top of the goal is defined by a crossbar, replacing strips of cloth that had been used up until then.
1877 England, where rules had not been used consistently, establishes a uniform structure. Suspension from the game is introduced.
1880 Following the British example, Germany adapts two

The Game of Soccer

30-minute halves (today it is two 45-minute halves).

1882 An international authority is established with a board that is responsible for settling all disputes.

1885 Professional soccer is born when England allows players to receive compensation.

1889 The referee, supported by two linesmen, is given unequivocal authority for game decisions. Until then, the game had two observers and one referee. The referee would only intervene when asked to do so by a team's leader.

1892 Betting on the outcome of a game between players and fans is outlawed.

1896 In Germany, the playing field has to be free of trees and bushes. Previously, natural obstacles were seen occasionally.

1900 The German Soccer Club is founded in Leipzig. Other soccer clubs were also established.

1902 England forbids women's soccer.

1903 An 18-yard (16-m) penalty area is established. The goalkeeper is only allowed to catch a ball in this zone.

1904 The International Soccer Association, FIFA, is founded in Paris. The concept of "dangerous play" is defined, and the free throw is introduced. The rule requiring shorts to cover the knees is finally abandoned.

1906 England joins the FIFA. The English rules are accepted internationally.

1907 A player is permitted to be offside in his own territory.

1921 Goalkeepers are required to wear yellow pullovers during international competition.

1924 Rules for corner kicks are revised. It is now possible to convert a corner kick directly.

1925 New offside rules make the game tactically more offensive. Only two opposing players need to be between the goal line and the attacker at the moment the attacker kicks the ball.

1929 New penalty-kick rules are adopted. The goalkeeper may not move until the kick is completed.

1933 For the British Cup Final, players wore their number on the back of their shirt. This rule was made official in 1938.

1951 By allowing the use of a white ball for night games, soccer enters the TV era.

1955 The ban on games played under floodlights is lifted.

1965 England allows the substitution of players in cases of injury.

1966 England permits substitution of two players, regardless of the reason.

1982 The four-step rule for the goalkeeper is adopted.

1985 Additional rules governing the goalkeeper's handling of the ball with his hands are enacted.

The original set of 17 rules established by the FIFA were grouped together as follows:

Requirements for the Game

Rule 1   The field of play
Rule 2   The ball
Rule 3   Number of players
Rule 4   Players' equipment

Guiding and Controlling the Game

Rule 5   The referee
Rule 6   The linesmen
Rule 7   Game duration

The Duration of Matches According to Gender, Age, and Location

Gender	Individual games outdoors		Competition played indoors			
	Age	Maximum duration	Age	Maximum duration	Overtime	Maximum playing time on any one day
Men	under 10 yrs 10–12 yrs 12–14 yrs 14–16 yrs 16–18 yrs over 18 yrs	two 20-min halves two 25-min halves two 30-min halves two 35-min halves two 40-min halves two 45-min halves	under 12 yrs under 18 yrs over 18 yrs	two 5-min halves two 10-min halves two 15-min halves	two 3-min periods two 3-min periods two 5-min periods	60 min 80 min 120 min
Women	under 10 yrs 10–13 yrs 13–16 yrs	two 25-min halves two 30-min halves two 35-min halves	under 16 yrs over 16 yrs	two 5-min halves one 10-min half	two 3-min periods two 3-min periods	60 min 80 min

The Game of Soccer

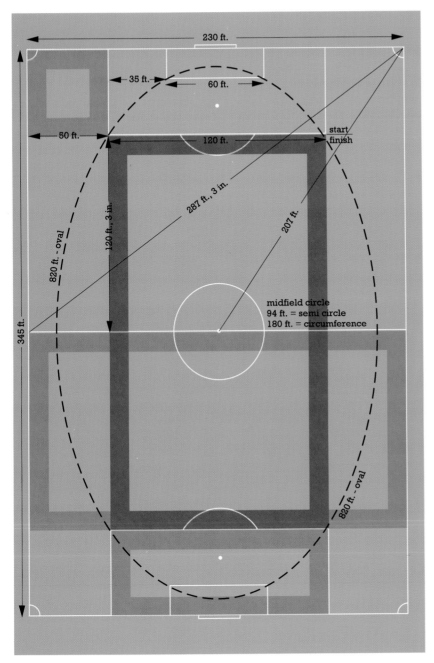

The standard-size playing field is 345 ft × 230 ft (105 × 70 m), divided into sections of varying dimensions in which specific training can take place. Together with permanent structures such as stairs and barriers, these areas offer a coach many possibilities for organizing and conducting varied training sessions. A skillful organizer can use the different sections of the field for numerous practice and game sessions.

Critical Game Situations
Rule 9   The ball in and out of play
Rule 10 Method of scoring
Rule 11 Offside
Rule 12 Fouls and misconduct

Standard Situations
Rule 13 Free kick
Rule 14 Penalty kick
Rule 15 Throw-in
Rule 16 Goal kick
Rule 17 Corner kick

The duration of matches involving women varies greatly. This has to be taken into consideration when designing a training program.

The Team

Part of the attraction that soccer has for so many players and spectators alike is that it is a team sport. Because of the number of players involved and the endless possibilities of offensive and defensive maneuvers, a player can let his imagination soar. The spectator is constantly treated to new and surprising combinations of plays.

Teamwork

The complex cooperation that is necessary for a team to be successful is the result of a combination of actions between two or more players and actions that involve the whole team.

Because of the many different types of action that players are involved in collectively, the effectiveness of a team is always more than the sum of the performance of 11 individual players. The game of a well-coached team often displays very special characteristics.

The Game of Soccer

Often these characteristics are influenced by a certain tradition particular to a club. In other words, a certain way of playing the game has been passed on from one generation to the next. In addition, some teams bear the very specific stamp of a successful coach who has a strong personality. The coach's idea of the most successful way of playing soccer becomes the hallmark of the team's play.

The character of a team is influenced by the following:

- The particular system being played (see page 137).
- The particular style of offense and defense (see page 143).
- The tactics used routinely by the members of the team (pages 91 and 97).
- The personalities of the different players of the team and their understanding of the game.

The Team as a Social Group

In psychological terms, the players of a team belong to a subgroup. A subgroup has specific characteristics, structures, and processes that are displayed between the members of the team or between the team and people on the outside. The coach occupies a position somewhat in between. The structure of a subgroup is influenced by the hierarchical order established among its members, which in turn is influenced by the relationship between them and their individual performance levels.

A clearly defined hierarchy, which is accepted by all members of the group, is absolutely essential. It eliminates infighting for position and jealousy. It establishes a leader who can inspire the team in critical situations and influence the team's enthusiasm and general level of performance.

In order for a soccer team to become a well-functioning subgroup, the following are helpful:

- During the course of a season, the number of players should remain constant, ideally between 18 and 25 members.
- All members should agree on a clearly defined goal (for instance, to prevent losing their position within a division or to move up in the standings).
- Players should agree on basic rules of conduct (for instance, to be on time for practice sessions and games).
- Players must have a well-developed team spirit.
- Players should accept their role within the hierarchical order of the group.
- Players should identify with, or at least accept, the person in charge (the coach or general manager of the club) or the institution they belong to.

Team-Building

It is an art to mould 11 individual people into a cohesive and powerful team. It is the job of the coach to establish a lineup based on the talents and strengths of each player. This process starts at the beginning of the season but it may extend over the course of several seasons until the players have been moulded into a solid team.

Whether putting together a lineup for one game or working on team development over the long run, a coach has to take a player's technical and tactical skills and his physical fitness into consideration. A coach also needs to evaluate a player's motivation and temperament. Furthermore, creativity and intuitiveness are important criteria a coach should consider when he makes decisions.

Soccer is not unlike music. Neither the violin nor the rhythmic section alone can convey the idea of a musical composition. It takes all of the individual members of an orchestra to express the idea. Orchestras need different players who are experts on their respective instruments.

And so it is in soccer: The strengths and talents of each player are needed to complement the whole. The tactician needs the fighter; the player developing a play needs the forward; a good offensive player in midfield needs someone he can count on for protection; a sweeper who is a weak header needs a player who is strong in that department; the somewhat slow-moving player in midfield position must be balanced by a defender who is explosively quick.

A coach needs to keep each player's abilities in mind as he puts his team together. In fact, a keen eye for the strengths and weaknesses of each player is the mark of a good coach. Often the absence of a particular type of player makes the difference between a successful and an average season.

Building a team over the long haul requires the following:

- Basically, the core of the team should consist of only as many players as necessary. Too little depth often causes problems when one of the regulars gets injured or when too many players leave at the same time. On the other hand, having too many players on the bench usually causes dissatisfaction, jealousy, and discord between players. A team should have two substitutes for each position. Since one player is usually capable of playing several positions, a roster of 18 to 22 players should be sufficient.

- The age of the players should be balanced. The productive years of a soccer player are between the ages of 20 and 32. The ideal age is between 24 and 28 years. A relatively young team often lacks the experience necessary during critical situations and often does not have sufficient stability and psychological maturity. However, if most of the team is too old, it might lack youthful fire and the willingness to take risks. During tournaments, it takes longer for older players to recuperate. Particularly in professional soccer, older players are often psychologically exhausted.
- Players, as was previously pointed out, should complement each other in technical and tactical skills and in physical fitness. Also, a team's particular style of play needs to be considered when looking for new players. A team that prefers frontal offense must have exceptional technicians in midfield. On the other hand, this team needs defenders that operate faster in open space than the opposing forwards. In reverse, the strikers of a counterattack team need to be exceptional sprinters.
- Players must have regard for each other as human beings. The world of sports is a wonderful example of how unimportant differences in race, religion, etc., are when the members of a group have the same goal. Everybody involved in the game

needs a certain amount of tolerance and life experience.
- Last, but not least, players must be able to accept the existing hierarchy of the team. A healthy competition among players is stimulating; intense rivalry for position causes problems.

The Lineup

When determining the lineup for a particular match, a coach also needs to consider the following:
- Don't tamper with success. It's usually wise to maintain a winning lineup.
- Players who are in a slump ought to be given a breather. On the other hand, a player should not be taken out of a lineup simply because he is not playing well on a given day. Ruthless substitutions breed insecurities over the long haul and remove the opportunity of making up for a weak performance.
- The lineup for a specific day may depend on the game tactics to be used against the particular opponent.
- The degree of participation and performance during training will also influence a lineup. A player who is lazy during training should be given a swift awakening by the coach so that the morale of the whole team isn't undermined.
- Finally, changes in the lineup are often the result of injuries or illnesses.

In the final analysis, only the coach knows all the factors that go into putting together a lineup. He should be the one to make the final decision.

The Player

Even though the team is more than the sum of all its players, each individual's performance determines the success and failure of the team. Over the course of a season, the team is also influenced by the personality of its players.

The Individual Player and the Team

Although it is not always clear to what extent the individual player is responsible for the success or failure of a team, a few ideas should be mentioned.

Obviously, a player's actions are most effective when he helps his side score a goal or prevents an opponent from scoring. For instance, a study by Jaschok/Witt (see page 11) of the frequency and duration of individual players' ball contacts showed a player with the shortest ball contact (20 seconds), during the 12 times he had possession of the ball, scored the deciding goal for a 1 to 0 win. Who could argue that the performance of this player was not significant for the team's success?

This also points up the fact that quantity (as measured by the distance covered in the course of a game) and quality of activities are not necessarily synonymous. For example, the action of a player who passes the ball to a teammate who then scores a goal is most certainly moving up the hierarchical ladder, just like a player who can prevent an opposing forward from scoring a goal.

Judging the importance of a positive action (for instance, completing a pass) or a negative action (incomplete pass) is also a matter

The Game of Soccer

of the space available for such actions. An unsuccessful pass away from the player's own goal is much more serious than losing the ball while dribbling in the opponents' penalty area. In the final analysis, the measure of a player's effectiveness lies in the ratio of his positive to negative actions.

Because the success of a team depends on the level of performance of each individual player, a coach must constantly work with his players to improve their level of performance and their readiness to perform.

Factors Influencing Performance

Many factors influence the daily performance of a player. The following are of particular importance:
- The player's overall characteristics.
- His natural talent.
- The degree of his technical and tactical skills and his physical fitness.
- His education.
- His life-style and nutrition.
- The attitude of his parents and friends.
- Pressures from school and job.
- The extent and quality of his previous training.

Some of these factors influence each other, some strengthen the effect on performance, and some cancel each other out. For instance, a player with only modest talent will improve his performance much more by a rigorous and intense training program than will a player who has great talent but little ambition.

Character Traits of a Star Player

In discussions of the future of the sport of soccer, we often hear the complaint that soccer is missing the presence of the big personalities, such as Pele, Beckenbauer, Netzer, Uwe Seeler, Fritz Walter, and others. A lack of skills and talent is, rather superficially, given as the reason. Not enough attention is paid to the fact that numerous character traits go into the making of a star personality. Conditioning, techniques, and tactics alone are not enough to be successful in competing in the international soccer arena or to be accepted as a star.

Personalities and, by extension, star players are shaped by the following:
- Personal characteristics such as gender and age.
- Physical attributes such as height and build.
- Intellectual abilities.
- Strength of motivation.
- Social skills.
- Attitudes and interests.
- Character traits and temperament.

Of course, some of these traits are natural gifts; however, many of them can be developed through an effective training program.

Personal Characteristics
Basic characteristics are:
- Age.
- Gender.
- Physical traits.

These factors influence performance. Because they cannot be changed or manipulated, a coach must take them into consideration.

Physical Traits
The important physical attributes are:
- Energy.
- Speed.
- Endurance.
- Mobility and flexibility.
- Coordination.

These characteristics appear in many different variations and in many different combinations. They are closely tied to motivational and emotional traits. They can be influenced to a certain degree by training, and we will discuss them in more detail in the chapter "Physical Fitness and Fitness Training."

Intellectual Abilities
The following are especially important:
- Perception.
- Concentration.
- Memory.
- Creativity.
- Anticipation (the ability to think ahead).
- Intuition.
- Abstract thinking.
- Judgment and knowledge.

More than anything else, these factors influence the tactical abilities of a player. Their importance and the possibility for improvement is discussed in more detail in the chapter on tactics.

Strength of Motivation
The following are some of the different motivational factors:
- The degree of desire to play the game and the need to excel.
- The desire for power or control.
- The need for acceptance.
- Emotions such as fear, anger, and pain.

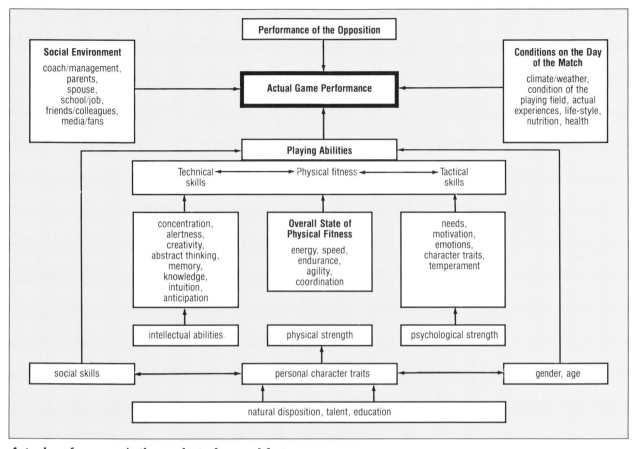

Actual performance is the product of several factors.

These characteristics play a large role in determining how a player uses his physical attributes. They can be influenced by a coach who employs the appropriate measures in his role as leader of the team.

Social Skills

Among other factors, these include the following:
- Acceptance of norms and values.
- Loyalty to the team.
- Willingness to be part of a team.
- Comradery.

These attributes develop over time. However, a coach's teaching methods can have a great impact.

Emotions and Temperament

The full range of emotions is part of a player's character. Examples are:
- Courage and fear.
- Decisiveness and indecisiveness.
- Impulsivity and caution.
- Aggression and passiveness.
- Self-confidence and insecurity.
- Extroversion and introversion.

These traits also influence a player's potential and performance as well as the place he occupies within the team. And here, too, a coach must try to nurture and develop those traits that can improve a player's performance (see page 89).

The factors that influence the level of performance of a player and the team have already been discussed in the section "Factors Influencing Performance" (see page 16). These factors can be guided, nurtured, developed, and improved through effective leadership and specific training methods. However, a coach must use consistent and systematic training that conforms to generally accepted methods. In order to achieve the desired results, the club management, the coach, and the players must work cooperatively, fulfilling their specific roles.

Responsibilities

Club Management

- Acquisition and care of equipment and facilities necessary for training: locker room, playing field, workout rooms and equipment, balls, on-site facilities for physical therapy and appropriate emergency medical care, and food and drink for the players.
- Providing appropriate personnel such as players, trainers, physician, massage therapist, grounds crew.

Trainer/Coach

The coach is responsible for preparing and overseeing the team's training schedule, as well as for setting goals, and for planning, conducting, and evaluating the effects of the training.

Players

The cooperation of the players determines the success of the training. Their contribution to a successful training program consists of the following:

- Maintaining an appropriate lifestyle.
- Establishing their own high performance standards.
- Cooperating during training.
- Taking responsibility for proper cool down (see page 156), making use of physical therapy, massages, and sauna.
- Following proper nutritional guidelines.
- Getting sufficient sleep.

Definitions and Principles

"Training" generally means all those activities that assure the improvement of performance. In sports, training usually means preparing for competition. This rather general definition only describes training's overall purpose and says very little about its concrete goals, tasks, and the effects of the training.

A more precise definition of soccer training states: Training is a methodically planned process for athletic perfection. The goal is to achieve optimal performance and readiness of the individual player and the team. Theoretical knowledge (general and specific training theories, biomechanics, sports medicine, sports psychology, and sports sociology) is as important as practical experience. Systematically repeated training results in physical and functional adaptation of the body.

This book has all the relevant information needed to establish a successful training program. The emphasis is on technical and tactical skills, physical conditioning, and all-around playing ability.

This chapter deals with the necessary, basic information and training theories. It sets the stage for the rest of the book. The reader will find specific information meant to deepen the understanding of the basics we have discussed so far.

In practical terms, both approaches to the training process, the general and the specific, are important. The complex effects of the training process can only be properly understood when the physical and the psychological effects are taken into consideration.

The fundamentals, which are the basis for the two approaches listed above, can be summarized as the concepts of training. They are:

- Teaching Principle (see below).
- Load Principle (see page 30).
- Cyclical Principle (see pages 34 and 35).

Teaching Principles

Principle of Methodical and Systematic Teaching

Training will only have the desired effects over the long haul when the methods chosen by the coach complement each other and are carried out systematically over a period of time (for instance, increasing the degree of difficulty). The prerequisite is a well-planned training program (see page 24).

Principle of Individuality and Age-Appropriateness

Training differs from player to player and from one developmental stage to the next. Optimum training results can only be achieved when the goal. the content, and the method of training are adjusted to the individual player.

Soccer Training

The degree of difficulty of the training program must be adjusted to the mental and physical abilities of the participants.

Principle of Clarity

Technical and tactical elements are learned and mastered much faster when the desired outcome of the training session is stated clearly. In addition, demonstrations, media photos, single and multiple slide presentations, and blackboard sketches are helpful in this attempt.

Principle of Awareness

Motivation, concentration, and performance improve when the players know what the outcome and the effects of an exercise are. Players should understand the connection between methods and outcome.

Type of Training

When people talk about soccer training, they often focus on improving performance. This book is oriented along these lines. However, in reality, depending on what a coach wants to accomplish, numerous other training methods are available.

Soccer Training in School

In school, soccer training is geared to do more than simply improve a player's performance. It includes many other, overriding responsibilities a school has to its students.

Soccer Training as Part of a Fitness Program

The main purpose is having fun. The therapeutic physiological ef-

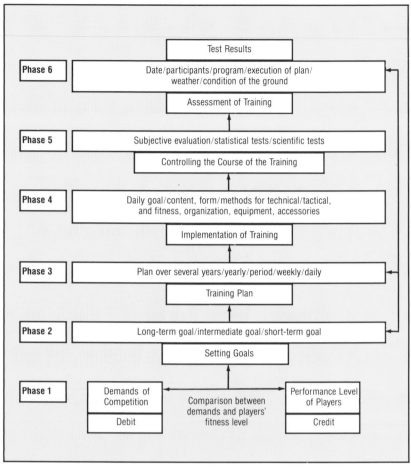

Different phases of the training program.

fects of the game are the reason for, not the goal of, training.

Soccer Training for Members of a Club

Here, the reason for training is the improvement of performance. Training programs are designed to that end.

Regrettably, all too often training for young and amateur players is modelled after the training program for professional players and is taken much too seriously. What is overlooked is the fact that training for professional players is a means to an end: to increase their level of performance, which will

ensure their income. Training has a totally different meaning for a professional than it does for young and amateur players (notwithstanding the fact that the latter make up 99.9 percent of all soccer players). For this reason, coaches must put aside their laudable athletic ambitions and develop training methods that will bring back a sense of fun. The idea is to turn away from grim and stubborn performance pressure, not from healthy ambition. Players need to be allowed to laugh during training sessions.

Performance-oriented training for young players is divided into three levels, depending on age and ability:

- Basic training: 6 to 10 years.
- Intermediate training: 12 to 14 years.
- Advanced training: 14 to 18 years.

Perhaps the most important statement in this book is:

> Each type and level of training has its specific requirements. Therefore, the goals, methods, exercises, and game plans of a training session must be chosen accordingly. Coaches must be quite careful when they are training children not to use carbon copies of training programs designed for adults.

The differences in age and development are evident in:
- The level of technical and tactical abilities and physical fitness.
- The approach and attitude towards a regular, consistent training program.
- The level of willingness to exert effort during training.
- The physical aptitude (a different "sensitive phase" exists for each level).
- The aptitude for coordinating specific motions and actions.
- The speed with which technical expertise is reached.
- The level of intellectual maturity.
- The ability to grasp instructions.
- The ability to translate instructions on tactics into practical game situations.

Concrete training goals for the different developmental stages of children and young people are summarized on page 23.

Different Phases of the Training Process

In the larger sense, training consists of more than just the work on the playing field. Training is a process of many phases that follow each other in a logical order; however, there is a constant interaction between them. The different phases are:
- Orientation.
- Establishing goals.
- Planning.
- Implementation.
- Checking progress.
- Evaluation.

Orientation Phase

As has been mentioned earlier, the requirements for competition vary widely and depend on the different performance and developmental stages of the players. Therefore, before converting a mental concept about a training program into concrete goals, a coach must first evaluate the demands a season of competitive games will make on the players and the team. This is the "debit." On the other hand, the coach has to evaluate the physical fitness of his players and his team. This is the "credit."

The soccer played by children and youth is vastly different from that played by professional adults. Of course, the same holds true for their technical and tactical abilities and for their physical condition. A coach must make decisions based on his players' and team's credit–debit situation in order to set goals and to develop an appropriate training program. Observation and evaluation of actual games and training sessions (perhaps with the help of video tapes and computer simulations)

help the coach determine the credit–debit balance of his team.

Establishing Training Goals

To ensure the successful outcome of a training session, it is vital for the objective to be proper and realistic. Without a clearly stated goal, a training session amounts to no more than activity therapy, and training can neither be planned nor carried out *systematically* this way.

Whether the objectives are long-term, intermediate, or short-term depends on the following:
- Age and state of development and maturity of the players.
- Level of performance of the players.
- Previous training.
- Philosophy and orientation of the coach and the players.
- Number of training periods set aside for practice in the course of the season.
- Day of the week set aside for practice.
- Realistic knowledge of the weaknesses of the players and the team.
- Environmental factors, such as the weather.
- Training facilities and equipment.

Senior Training Goals
As far as the training of senior players is concerned, training goals vary little from one year to the next; rather, they should vary within a season (see page 24). For a season divided into two halves, several weekly subdivisions should be established:
- Preparation.
- First round of competition.
- Interim period (winter break).
- Second round of competition.

Soccer Training

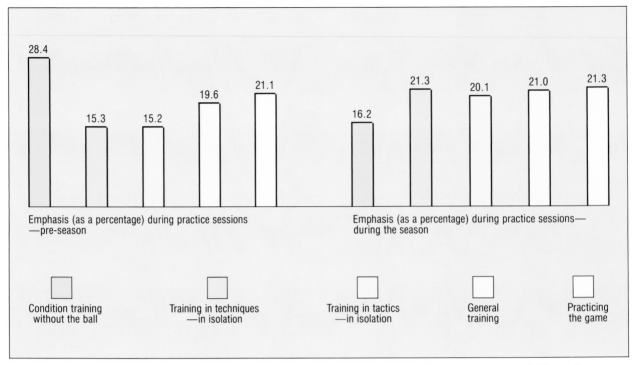

28.4   15.3   15.2   19.6   21.1   16.2   21.3   20.1   21.0   21.3

Emphasis (as a percentage) during practice sessions —pre-season

Emphasis (as a percentage) during practice sessions—during the season

Condition training without the ball   Training in techniques —in isolation   Training in tactics —in isolation   General training   Practicing the game

The relationship between different phases during practice sessions, according to a survey of 59 coaches.

- Interim period (break without training or practice).

Scientific studies have proven, and practical experience has confirmed, that neither a player nor a team can maintain levels of high performance consistently over several seasons.

The performance of a player moves from one distinct level to another and is subject to the biological reactions and functions of the human body. The levels are:
- Increase in the level of performance.
- Peak level of performance.
- Declining level of performance.

The first objective of a training program, therefore, is to establish *the degree of the training load*. This goal can be realized by adhering to the training principles outlined (see page 30).

The second objective should be to determine *the balance between the training in terms of techniques, tactics, and physical conditioning*. (See bar chart illustrating the results of a survey of 59 coaches in all classes.)

The third objective is to decide on the desired *goal of a training program*. The emphasis on techniques, tactics, and physical conditioning will change, depending on the goal. The objectives of training vary within different phases of a program.

Objectives of a Junior Training Program

The objectives of a training program for juniors depend on the developmental stage of the players. At this age, growth spurts are often rapid and take place in varying degrees. These are factors a coach must take into consideration when establishing a training program. Training manuals talk about "sensitive phases." These are the times particularly suited for the development of specific talents, abilities, and skills.

If a training program doesn't take advantage of these developmental periods, it is almost impossible to make up for them later—at least this is the general consensus of opinion. For the same reason, specialization or a soccer-specific training program should not be undertaken too early. Basic training sessions should give young players the opportunity to gain experience in running and movement-related exercises. (See the section on coordination and coordination training on page 82).

In addition, long-term training objectives for youth programs as well as for senior training are influenced by dividing practice sessions into specific phases. The following tables are divided into specific age groups. The training objectives are based on the knowl-

Establishing Age-Appropriate Training Objectives

To be accomplished	6–10 years	10–12 years	12–14 years	14–16 years	16–18 years
Sustain enjoyment of playing and practicing	Enjoying playing with the ball without fear—rolling, jumping, and kicking	Enjoying cooperative play, learning to play, enjoying practice	Enjoying one-on-one competition and competing together to win	Gaining satisfaction and enjoyment from the improvement of own performance and understanding what that means to the team	Enjoying performance-oriented practice of tactics, techniques, and conditioning. "Soccer forever!"
Coordination (general)	Learning to anticipate movement of the ball; motor skills (general)	Improving coordination of ball and body movement; gaining a "feel" for the ball	Strengthening overall motor skills and general dexterity, despite rapid growth spurt at this age	Improving body control during one-on-one confrontations; developing toughness in the face of an opponent's attack	Improving agility when under pressure and despite an opponent's attack
Specific technical abilities	Ball control: simple forms of fielding and handling; instep goal kicking	All basic forms of movement and techniques with and without an opponent	Finetuning basic form; simulating actual game situations	Position-specific techniques; improving dribbling and tackling in one-on-one situations	Using techniques to accomplish objectives (free kick, corner kick); learning to consciously use techniques when moving fast and when involved in one-on-one confrontations
General and specific conditioning	Running, jumping, leaping, and rolling; endurance and agility during play	Improving quickness and coordination by running, playing rough-and-tumble games, and running relays	Improving endurance and motor skills through extensive running and exercises (gymnastics)	Beginning general as well as specific muscle training; practice to improve speed and aerobic strength	Training to improve jumping and kicking skills, aerobic endurance, strength of body muscles, and specific speed with and without the ball
Knowledge and implementation of tactical skills	Understanding what "scoring a goal", and "avoiding a goal" and "coordinated offense and defense" mean	Playing within a designated space and learning to deal with the typical situations that develop there; individual tactics (getting free, coverage)	Improving teamwork (group tactics); practicing the tactically correct reaction to standard situations	Knowledge of tactics used during games; improving individual actions as part of team tactics (offensive, defensive, space coverage)	Independent, and responsible, execution of tactical maneuvers; application of all personal skills
Knowledge of rules	Knowledge of rudimentary rules: scoring a goal, throw-in, fouls and misconduct, offside	Adhering to all rules, especially Rule 4 and Rules 8 through 17	Acceptance of the ruling of a referee	Readiness to referee a game	Ability to organize and referee games
Teaching self-realization through play					
Willingly increasing level of performance during practice as well as during a game	Learning through personal effort to translate various game strategies into action during rough-and-tumble play and running	Converting enjoyment of the game and excess energy into action on the field; after proper instruction, practicing training exercises independently	Overcoming feelings of reluctance and negative performances (those that are developmentally influenced); understanding and accepting that the success of the team is more important than any one individual's success	Striving to raise the personal level of performance by working on tactics, techniques, and fitness (avoiding alcohol, tobacco, etc.)	Combining school and other interests with athletic goals; developing additional motivation
Control of effect and aggression	Accepting the fact that losing is part of the game and that "tomorrow is another day"	Learning to experience and control joy, anger, and rage	Developing toughness in one-on-one confrontations; learning to tolerate pain	Learning to handle rivalries and aggression	Developing psychological stability; learning to control competition-induced anxiety and nervousness
		Learning to accept the decision of the referee			
Develop team spirit and socially acceptable conduct	See soccer in terms of teamwork during games and practices	Learn to share tasks with a group or team; establish friendships	See the team as a group of people with the same goals, interests, and standards; respect the opponent	Learn to fit into the team's hierarchy; see the team (including the coach) as a group involved in competitive performances	See the team as part of larger unit (school or club); be loyal to that unit
Learn to organize games and training programs	Learn to follow coach's instructions; fulfill responsibilities	Participate in organizing the training program; set up groups and handling equipment	Learn to organize training objectives and adjust exercise programs accordingly	Participate in and help organize practice sessions; train independently; evaluate own progress by checking achievements	Actively participate in and contribute to the success of all team activities; actively contribute to scheduling training and practice sessions

Soccer Training

edge and experiences gained from practical situations.

Specific goals for teaching technical and tactical skills and for physical conditioning are discussed in more detail in their respective chapters.

Training Schedule

Because of the variety of training objectives a coach can choose from and the difficulty in regulating the physical stress involved, a coach must have a written training schedule.

> A training schedule is the translation of a mental concept that states systematically the actual structure and objectives of a training program.

This concept may be written down or displayed in graphic form and may include periods of differing length. For soccer the following schedules are used:
- Schedules and plans covering several years for the development of a team with young players.
- Yearly training schedule for junior and senior players.
- Schedules for different periods of a season: pre-season, competition, interim and transition period.
- Weekly practice schedules.
- Daily practice schedules.

The shorter the time period covered by a schedule, the more concise the description of the exercises has to be. It is not enough to plan the actual objectives and the degree of the training load.

A yearly schedule, for example, must include the following:
- Objectives (for instance, moving up in the standings).

Example of a Training Schedule for a Senior Team for One Year

1. Period: mid-July to mid-August

Type of training	a. Intensity b. Extent	Training goals	Training exercises
General conditioning training; fundamentals of fitness training; repetition of fundamental techniques and tactics	a. 60–80% b. 80–100%	**Conditioning** Aerobic endurance, general power training; agility **Techniques** Repetition of all technical skills; practice sessions for individual players **Tactics** General and individual tactical skills: getting free, coverage, dribbling; basic tactics in standard situations: free kick, corner kick, different combinations, changing positions	Running, jogging, gymnastics Game plays, exercises, individual training with ball, training in specific and specialty skills Individual work on frontal attack, team attack; practical and board exercises

2. Period: mid- to end of August

| Soccer-specific conditioning training; improvement of specific physical conditioning and technical and tactical skills | a. increase to 95%
b. reduce to 60% | **Conditioning**
Aerobic stamina, general power exercises, special skills
Techniques
All elements with opponent and increased tempo
Tactics
Team training, assigning positions, trying out new game strategies | Extensive interval training, running relay races with and without a ball, abbreviated games, general soccer games (offense/defense)
Complex exercises: one-on-one, short soccer games with special assignments
Game play: offense against defense, practice game with "weaker" opponent; discussions, board exercises |

3. Period: end of August to mid-September

| Soccer-specific reinforcement of complex skills, making them "automatic" | a. 90–100%
b. reduce from 100% to about 50% | **Conditioning**
Highest possible reaction and speed skills; jumping and kicking power
Techniques
Perfect coordination of technical elements and physical fitness
Tactics
Technical and tactical exercises appropriate to a given situation; changing tempo, speed, and positions | Practicing all soccer-specific exercises with highest possible speed
Game plays with players assuming different positions, practicing being outnumbered and outnumbering the opposition
Practicing different tactics against weaker opponent |

- Dividing the year into different time periods and phases.
- Dates of the championship games.
- Dates of exhibition games.
- Date and type of tests and physical examinations.
- In rough form, a statement of objectives for techniques, tactics, and physical fitness.
- Amount of time set aside for each objective.
- Degree of load, particularly the ratio between extent and intensity of training during each period.

The following tables give examples of a one-year schedule for senior players. The basic concept of "training load" in the course of a season is easy to detect.

A written schedule of a training program is like a signpost, serving as a general guide throughout the year. However, a coach is not expected to adhere rigidly to such a schedule. Anything can happen, so it's wise to be flexible. This is another reason why it is helpful to have a general outline that covers an extended period of time. The rationale for dividing a year into different periods is discussed in more detail on page 34.

The suggested schedule, outlined on pages 24 through 27, covers one year.

4. Period: mid-September to mid-October

Type of training	a. Intensity b. Extent	Training goals	Training exercises
Soccer-specific program and additional, unrelated exercises	a. 90–100% b. increase from 80 to 90%	**Conditioning** Increase training load by increasing intensity of exercises **Techniques** Using all technical elements at the highest speed possible in game-like situations against "opponents" **Tactics** Developing "real-game" tactical skills, learning from the experiences of past competitions	Increase in the number and duration of practice sessions, shorten duration of timeouts Basketball, handball, general power training (once a week)

5. Period: mid-October to mid-November

| Decrease in intensity to aid recuperation and prevent loss of form | a. reduce from 100 to 70%
b. approximately 50% | **Conditioning**
Extended and intermediate endurance, agility training; no speed or power-endurance training
Techniques
Perfect all technical elements using moderate running speed (high number of repetitions)
Tactics
Improving tactics in standard situations | Stretching exercises (gymnastics); endurance training (jogging, soccer-tennis); practice games, increasing the number of players, using a variety of game strategies; no intense one-on-one competition, rather increasing the number of repetitions |

6. Period: mid-November to mid-December

| Balanced training exercises utilizing many different types of sports to maintain psychological readiness | a. increase to 80%
b. continue decrease (fewer, but more intensive, training sessions) | **Conditioning**
Work on basic motor skills: increased power, speed, and reaction time
Techniques
Increase in general athletic skills, agility, and dexterity
Tactics
Game comprehension; enjoyment of the game and good humor | Abbreviated rough-and-tumble games, abbreviated soccer games, table tennis, volleyball, basketball, and handball

Complex exercises: practicing offense against defense, practice games against weaker opponents |

7. Period: mid-December to mid-January: no training

Soccer Training

8. Period: mid-January to end of January			
Type of training	a. Intensity b. Extent	Training goals	Training exercises
General power training (beginning in January); few, but very intensive, training sessions	a. increase from 80 to 100% b. moderate, approximately 50–70%	**Conditioning** Soccer-specific short endurance training, reaction speed **Techniques** Ball-body coordination, one-on-one competitions **Tactics** Direct pass and double pass alternating with dribbling and combination plays	Intensive interval exercises, including game methods: abbreviated games, one-on-one competition Indoor training with broken plays

9. Period: end of January to mid-February			
For beginning amateur teams: preparation for return matches; for advanced amateur teams and professional teams: strengthen form	for beginners: a. increase to 100% b. 70–80% for advanced: a. decrease to 80% b. increase to 90%	**Conditioning** Basic speed, jumping and kicking power, action and reaction training; training in the beginning: high-intensity and longer timeouts, followed by lower-intensity and shorter timeouts **Techniques** Long passes, long kicks (ground with snow cover), driving the ball with speed **Tactics** Utilizing space, changing sides, changing tempo, alternating between offensive and defensive plays	In contrast to Period 7, increased number of training sessions and increased duration of individual sessions, followed by extensive interval training Complex exercises: practice games, eight-on-eight, using the whole field; game using four goals alternating between three teams

10. Period: mid-February to mid-April			
Intense training sessions, going through microcycles to maintain good form; motivate for the final "push"	a. 80% b. 40–50%	**Conditioning** Train to increase endurance (aerobic, anaerobic), later add power endurance; improve basic motor skills, speed, and strength in general **Techniques** As close to "real game" situations as possible: all elements of complex techniques **Tactics** Observing tactical skills of individual players during game practice and work to improve them in training	First extensive and then intensive interval training; increase number of game plays; increased discussions with individual players to raise level of motivation for the "final push"

Today, coaches often plan the content and intensity of training sessions with the team captain.

11. Period: mid-April to mid-May			
Type of training	a. Intensity b. Extent	Training goals	Training exercises
This will depend to a great extent on the standing of the team. If in the middle of the pack, goal-specific training of individual players	a. approximately 70% b. approximately 50%	**Conditioning** Reducing the intensity in order to maintain good form over time; high duration of training **Techniques** Improvement of technical skills through individual and specialized training **Tactics** Improvement of individual tactical skills, training in fundamental tactical skills (combination drills, double pass, etc.)	Recuperation through aerobic exercises (distance running); gymnastics (exercising with a partner), rough-and-tumble games, soccer-tennis, abbreviated games in a small group with relatively low intensity (three-on-one, four-on-two, etc.) Establish training programs for individual players and initiate individual exercise sessions

12. Period: mid-May to June			
Total relaxation, but under no circumstances total inactivity	a. reduce to 50% b. reduce to 70%	**Conditioning** Regeneration and rejuvenation **Techniques** Recapture the fun of the game **Tactics** Increase knowledge of tactical skills through literature and the like	General physical checkup by physician; undergoing treatment (surgery) if necessary Alternative athletic activities: hiking, mountain climbing, tennis, table tennis, and on a smaller scale, swimming, sauna and massage therapy; ball practice alone to improve technical weaknesses

Implementation of a Training Program

The following didactical components should be considered when planning a training schedule:
- Actual objectives of the training.
- Training method.
- Training content (game plays, exercises, complex exercises, training games).
- Organization of training sessions (type of structure, assignments, equipment, and accessories).

Daily Training Objectives

The immediate training objectives depend in part on the previously established long-term and intermediate goals. In addition, information gathered during prior competitions about individual players and the team as a whole plays a role in the decisions. Short-term objectives depend on unforeseen, external conditions (such as rain, muddy grounds, and snow).

One goal, however, should always be part of a coach's daily schedule: "to play, to laugh, and to have fun!" A good coach understands that this attitude does not diminish his commitment to serious, performance-oriented training sessions.

Training Methods

Today, the three areas of performance—techniques, tactics, and conditioning—are usually taught by using real-game situations in the form of game plays or training games.

Soccer Training

This is important, because children of today, in contrast to earlier generations, don't play street soccer very often.

Clubs committed to competitive sports have specific methods for training. We distinguish between the following methods:
- Technical training (page 60).
- Tactical training (page 88).
- Fitness training (page 68).

To a great extent, experts agree on the best methods for training in fitness and tactics. However, opinions differ over the most effective training methods for the techniques necessary for the development of total athletic skills. A discussion of the pros and cons of the technical training methods used most often can be found on pages 60 through 62.

Type of Training

The type and content of training is influenced by the following:
- The training objectives.
- The anticipated training load.
- The training method chosen.
- The levels of development and performance of the players.
- The interests and the motivation of the players.
- The available space and equipment (for instance, the number of soccer balls).

The following sets of exercises are important for soccer training:
- General conditioning without the ball.
- Rough-and-tumble games.
- Individual, self-generated exercises to develop a "feel" for the ball.
- Exercises with a partner, standing and moving.
- Game strategies and combinations.
- Complex exercises.
- Small game plays.
- Training games, 11-on-11.

Significance of Different Methods for Training Techniques Based on Age and Developmental Level

	Developmental or age level				
	6–10 years	10–12 years	12–14 years	14–16 years	16–18 years
General conditioning without a ball	–	O	O	OO	OO
Rough-and-tumble games	OO	OO	OO	O	O
Independent exercises to improve ball handling	OOO	OOO	OO	OO	OO
Exercising with a partner, standing and moving	OOO	OO	OO	O	O
Competition exercises, one-on-one exercises	O	OO	OO	OOO	OOO
Strategy games, different combination plays	O	OO	OO	OO	OO
Complex exercises	–	O	OO	OOO	OOO
Small game plays	OOO	OOO	OO	OO	OO
Training games	OOO	OOO	OOO	OO	O

– not important   O important   OO very important   OOO extremely important

Individual sets of exercises can be combined, resulting in different physical conditioning. The significance of individual types of exercises to increase the level of performance is displayed in the table on page 28.

Organizing a Training Schedule

The choice of methods and types of exercises has a significant impact on how training sessions are organized. To a great extent, these choices determine the success of the total training program as well as the accomplishment of the objectives the team has set for itself.

There is a close connection between the training load (which needs to be at a certain level for long-term performance to increase) and the way a training program is organized. A maximum training load can only be reached if the transition from one training phase to another is as smooth as possible. The transition should not unintentionally increase the load.

When organizing a schedule, the following aspects should be taken into consideration:
- Dividing the players into specific groups (type of division).
- Assigning playing space to each group.
- Alternating the groups between different types of exercise and from one space to another.
- Duration of individual exercises and of training games.
- Frequency, duration, and type of break.
- Providing the necessary equipment and accessories.

- Considering the condition of the grounds and the permanent structures (buildings, stairs, barriers) in a stadium or playing field when making decisions.

Checking Achievement of Objectives

It is not always easy to determine if the goals of a training program have been reached. Because the levels of soccer performance are so varied, it is possible that while an individual player shows definite improvement, the result can only be marginally documented because the overall team performance fell short of expectations.

Additionally, coaches often overlook improved performance of players on the bench. These problems can be eliminated with controls for checking specific training objectives. These controls can be established using the following methods:

- Subjective evaluation of a player's improved performance during training sessions and competition.
- Objective tests measuring athletic-specific motor activities.
- Scientific tests to measure performance.

Subjective Evaluation of Improved Performance by the Coach

Over time, experienced coaches develop a rather good eye for a player's level of technical performance and physical fitness. They usually have sufficient distance from the activity of a given game or training situation to analyze a performance objectively. However, these evaluations will always remain somewhat subjective, and this method does not stand up to critical scrutiny. As long as the coach and his team are successful, no specific evaluation methods are necessary; however, when failures accumulate, the evaluation methods of a coach are quickly drawn into question.

Objective Motor-Activity Tests

Sports science has developed sev-

There are many ways to test technical skills. For comparison purposes, the exercises must be standardized.

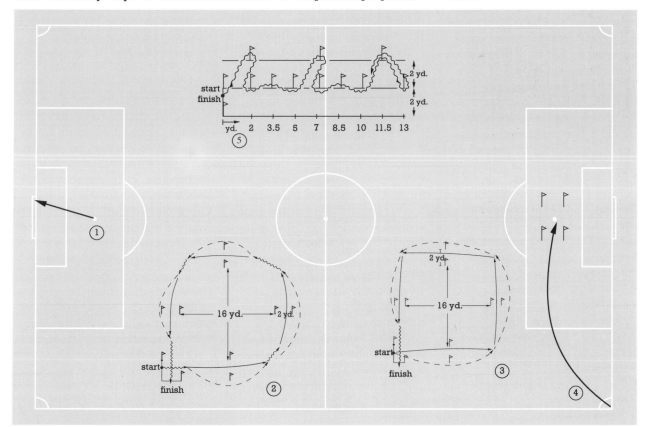

Positions from which to test technical skills:
1. Goalkicking test   2. Dribbling-pass test   3. Passing-timing test   4. Goalkicking test from the side   5. Dribbling test

Soccer Training

eral methods to objectively test the level of performance of a player. They are:

- Testing the level of technical skills (see diagram below).
- Testing the level of physical conditioning as seen in the quality of athletic skills.

Sports science has also developed methods to objectively test the parameters of tactical skills; however, at this time, they do not have great relevance for training purposes. In order for a test to render useful information, it is imperative that it meets the following criteria:

A test must be *valid*. It must measure what it professes to measure. For instance, a slalom course certainly does not measure dribbling skills—many more factors play a role in that activity.

A test must be *reliable*. The instruments used for the test must be accurate and used properly, and the order in which the test is given must be appropriate.

A test must be *objective*. Instructions for the implementation, analysis, and interpretation of the test must be clearly stated so that the results can be used independently.

Scientific Measurements

Increasingly, professional soccer uses performance-level tests that have been developed by sports medicine. Those best known are:

- Spiro-ergonomic measurements on the treadmill or bicycle, and lactic-acid measurements.
- Lactic-acid test after sprints or after jogging around the field.
- Uric-acid test.
- Computerized power-energy measurements.

Spiro-ergonomic measurements give information about cardiovascular efficiency (intake and utilization of oxygen). Lactic-acid measurements before and after a workout provide information about aerobic and anaerobic limits (see page 75). Uric-acid measurements after a workout yield information about the degree of fatigue. These measurements make it possible to design subsequent training sessions with the proper physical loads.

Computer-guided energy measurements are able to determine the degree of energy deficit. This might be used after an injury. By following the curves on a graph, experienced analysts can even detect hidden muscle damage.

Evaluation of a Training Program

A careful analysis of training sessions has long-term benefits for several reasons. With a written account, the coach is able to review and establish the following:

- Which players took part in a given training session; how often each player practised.
- What kind of skills were practised at what time.
- What was the extent and intensity of an individual training session and of the whole season.
- To what degree did the long-term training schedule correspond to the results obtained.
- What kind of weather conditions existed during any given practice session.
- The test results.

A coach can make up his own forms for record keeping; however, for the sake of simplicity, a coach can buy training forms for that purpose at many sports stores.

Guiding the Training Load

Principles of Training Load

Training manuals and practical experience have established the connection between:

Load—Recuperation— Adaptation

and formulated the following principles:

- A physical load, exceeding the absolute threshold of an individual player, will decrease substances such as hormones and enzymes in a player's system and, consequently, lead to fatigue (see page 74 concerning the significance of energy availability).
- Depending on the type and amount of a load, these substances decrease in different degrees, showing specific symptoms of fatigue.
- The duration of fatigue depends on the type and degree of the fatigue. Even well-trained athletes may show symptoms for up to three days (72 hours) after the event.
- Essential substances, depleted during a workout, are replaced at an accelerated rate with nutrition appropriate for an athlete. This biological phenomenon, called the *principle of hyper-compensation*, helps develop the desired musculature and metabolic adaptation when combined with fitness training.
- According to the *principle of optimum correlation* of stress load to recuperation, the next training session should take place within 12 to 72 hours, at the peak of the hyper-compensation process.

Duration of Fatigue and Recuperation Depending on the Type of Training Stress Load (Keul 1978, Kindermann 1978, Martin 1980)

Training stress load / Recuperation	For aerobic energy availability (training with low-intensity stress load)	For combined aerobic-anaerobic energy availability (training with average stress-load intensity)	For anaerobic energy availability (speed and power exercises, competition)	For anabolic effects (maximum power training)	For affecting the neuromuscular system (speed training, techniques training, competition)
Ongoing recuperation	With an intensity of 60–70%, recuperation is ongoing				With a short training load (according to the repetition method) and longer timeouts
Quick recuperation (very incomplete)		After approximately 1½ to 2 hours	After approximately 2 to 3 hours		
90–95% recuperation (incomplete with good performance capacity)	After 12 hours with a 75–90% intensity	After approximately 12 hours	After approximately 12–18 hours	After approximately 18 hours	After approximately 18 hours
Total recuperation of the balance between metabolic processes (increased performance capacity)	After 24–26 hours with a 75–90% intensity	After approximately 24–28 hours	After approximately 48–72 hours	After approximately 72–84 hours	After approximately 72 hours

- According to the *principle of varying stress load*, if training sessions with high stress loads are scheduled in rapid succession (for instance, daily exercise sessions), different training objectives should be established, resulting in a different fatigue process (for instance, endurance, energy, and central nervous system).
- Increasing the level of performance during competition can only be achieved by increasing the physical stress load. According to the *principle of increased stress load*, this can be accomplished by using the following methods:
- Establishing a gradual, linear training program for beginners and advanced players.
- Rapid, multi-stage types of performance training.
- Variations of the above.

Components of Stress-Load Training

From the prior discussion, it is clear that a training program can only be successful by designing and using a systematic training stress load. The means for aiding this process are the so-called "training stress-load components."

Stimulus Intensity

The intensity of an individual training stimulus is 100 percent whenever the stress load is so high that only one more repetition of a given activity (such as pressing weights) can be accomplished. For running, 100 percent intensity is reached when a player is sprinting at his fastest possible speed. To develop maximum energy and maximum speed, the training stress load must reach maximum intensity (or at least come close to it). This is only possible with sufficiently long intervals between individual training stimuli.

Stimulus Density

Stimulus density is the relationship between the stress load and the recuperation phase. When the stimulus intensity is low, stimulus

Soccer Training

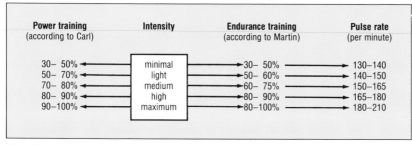

Power training (according to Carl)	Intensity	Endurance training (according to Martin)	Pulse rate (per minute)
30– 50%	minimal	30– 50%	130–140
50– 70%	light	50– 60%	140–150
70– 80%	medium	60– 75%	150–165
80– 90%	high	80– 90%	165–180
90–100%	maximum	80–100%	180–210

Ranking the Intensity of a Training Stress Load (including subjective impressions)

density may be maximized, which means that training can be almost continuous, as, for instance, during jogging.

Stimulus Duration

The duration of one stimulus, or of a series of stimuli (for instance, during interval training), is also a factor. The duration of the stimulus is too long during speed training if the player is unable to sprint at maximum intensity. Training should then be directed more to speed endurance rather than maximum speed.

Degree of Stimulus

The degree of stimulus is a combination of duration and number of stimuli per training session and is primarily independent of the intensity of the individual stimulus. Since there is a maximum training-load limit, the degree and intensity cannot be decreased independently.

Exercise Frequency

From practical experience as well as research in sports science, we know that training is more effective (given the identical training stress load) when it occurs frequently and is less extensive, as compared to less frequent and

more extensive exercises. For this reason it is useful to increase the number of training sessions during the pre-season period. Even three sessions a day will not be too much if the intensity of each individual session is not too high, and if the objectives and the content are changed regularly.

Physical fitness (form) is improved when there is a balance between duration and intensity, and when the training program is spread over several training sessions. This balance plays an important role in the management of the training as a whole and in dividing a training program into several periods.

Methods for Stress-Load Training

Four very different methods for stress-load training are relevant to the management of stress loads. Each one distinguishes itself by a specific balance between extent, duration, intensity, and frequency.

Every method has a different effect on the body. It is possible to accomplish two essential objectives by a systematic, goal-directed application of these methods:

- Skills dependent on physical fitness, energy, speed, and endurance can be realized

independently by systematic training (see page 34).

- The psycho-physiological performance ability can be influenced. This fact has important implications for the division of the training program into individual periods (see page 34).

Constant Method (CM)

The constant method (divided into CM I—up to 30 minutes, CM II—up to 60 minutes, and CM III—over 60 minutes) can improve almost all aerobic endurance. This is accomplished only if the density of the stress load is high, meaning nonstop training with no timeouts. The duration of the stimuli should be at least 20 minutes. For physically fit athletes the intensity should be high enough that the pulse rate is raised to 160–170 (CM I), 150–160 (CM II), and 140 to 150 (CM III) beats per minute. The constant method is used extensively during the practice season. However, since we know that aerobic endurance training must take place on a regular basis during active competition as well, it is useful to include a training session using the CM method once a week during active competition.

It is very important not to exceed a moderate jogging speed. Experience has shown that coaches and players alike want to run too fast. This interferes with the desired adaptation process (for instance, an increase in the rate at which carbohydrates and fats are burned). In soccer, the constant training method is used to practise techniques (for example, standard combinations). Game plays with five-on-five or eight-on-eight are ideal, because the ball remains in play all the time. This keeps breaks short and rest periods to a minimum.

Stress-Load Method: Extent and Ratio of Stress Components; Goals of Fitness Training and Performance Control

Method	Stress load during endurance training (running)	Stress load during power and energy training	Training goal	Performance control
Prolonged method	E: 70–100% I: 30–50% B: none PR: 140–160	Not applicable for power training; not effective with low intensity	General, long-term aerobic endurance	Increasing productivity during pre-season
Examples:	Continuous ball exercises (no breaks); eight-on-eight			
Extensive interval method	E: 3–5 series, jogging 4–10 times each, over 50–150 feet (20–50 m) I: 60–70% B: 1–2 minutes PR: 160–170/140	E: 2–5 series, 10–20 times each I: 40–60% B: 30–90 seconds	Mixed aerobic and anaerobic endurance; maximum energy endurance for increasing energy and power	To maintain productivity during competition
Examples:	Examples: Changing tempo during jogging and training games; three-on-three up to six-on-six or three-plus-three-on-two			
Intensive interval method	E: 4–6 series of 2–5 runs each I: 80–90% B: 2–4 minutes PR: 170–180/120	E: 4–6 series, 6–10 times each I: 55–75% B: 2–5 minutes	Anaerobic endurance and stamina; explosive speed; kicking-shooting power	Rapid increase in productivity
Examples:	Sprints over 15–100 yards (5–30 m); one-on-one; training games one-on-one or two-on-two			
Repetition method	E: 3 series repeated 1–5 times I: 90–100% B: 2–5 minutes PR: 180–200/80–100	E: 3–5 series, 1–5 times I: 70–100% B: 3–5 minutes PR: 180–220/80	Speed; maximum power	Increase in productivity; maintaining productivity
Examples:	Sprints over 50–300 feet (50–100 m); one-on-one			
Competition method	Training and competition games			Near perfection
E: Extent, I: Intensity, B: Break, PR: Pulse Rate during activity/after break				

Interval Method (IM)

The interval training method uses the systematic exchange between stress and recuperation. Depending on the intensity of the stress load and its duration and the intensity of the stimulus influenced by it, we distinguish between two types of interval methods:

• The extensive interval method.
• The intensive interval method.

Breaks are relatively short and can be actively used for gymnastics or light ball exercises ("productive breaks"). Circle training, where different types of exercises are carried out consecutively in different areas (circles), lends itself well to interval training.

During general conditioning training, it is also possible to improve physical strength by skillfully combining the exercises with endurance training. In soccer-specific interval-method training, groups of players constantly alternate between games and breaks. The primary emphasis is on techniques, tactics, and skills combined with physical conditioning.

Repetition Method

The repetition method also uses constant, alternating periods of recuperation and exercise; however, active periods are conducted with maximum intensity and scheduled timeouts are longer than those used with the interval method. Exercise is not resumed until the pulse rate is back to approximately

Soccer Training

80 beats per minute. An example of interval-method training would be 50 to 100 sprints alternating with timeout periods.

Usefulness of Training Methods

The intensity of the stress load is different for each of the above training methods. Also, the effect of the intensity of the individual methods (exercises and games) is different. Therefore, stress-load training can only be effective if the proper training method is chosen. The table on this page lists training methods, grouped according to their different degrees of intensity.

Training Methods with Different-Intensity Stress Loads

Method suitable for	Examples of training method
Constant method—jogging, low-intensity, aerobic-endurance training	Jogging, gymnastics and stretching; techniques and self-generated exercises, running techniques, and combination plays in two or three groups; three-on-one, four-on-two, nine-on-nine
Extensive interval method—high-intensity, mixed aerobic-endurance training	Running with changing tempo, circular training, intensive movement gymnastics, one-on-one exercises, technique training at moderate running tempo, double-pass exercises, complex exercises, games with six-on-six to eight-on-eight, games with four goals on goal line, games involving being outnumbered and outnumbering attack on defense
Intensive interval method—high-intensity, anaerobic-endurance training	Relay races with and without a ball, running with increasing tempo, sprints of 15–150 yards (5–50 m); games of two-on-two up to seven-on-seven, games of one-plus-one-on-one and one-plus-two-on-two, games of three-on-two and two-on-two
Repetition method with maximum intensity	Running in hilly terrain, hurdle jumping, workout on stairs and power equipment, jumping down; games of one-on-one until (subjectively) exhausted

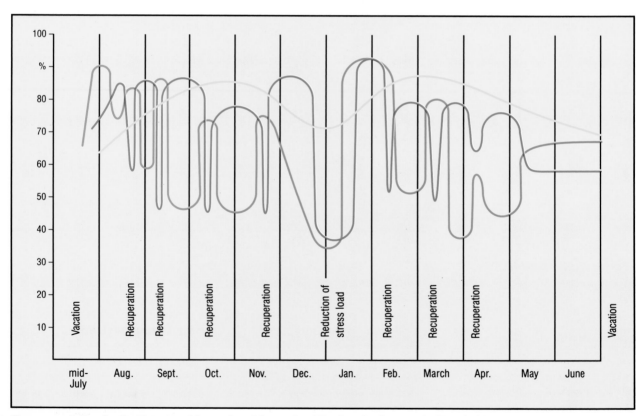

Recommendation for the Extent and Intensity of Stress Load During the Course of a Year (with two 4-week vacation periods: July/August and December/January)

———— **Blue: Extent**
———— **Red: Intensity**
———— **Yellow: Desired Curve**

Dividing Training Schedules into Periods

In the section on stress loads, we outlined the principles of the optimum relationship between stress load and recuperation. These principles hold true for the individual training periods (those periods that don't follow one another in succession). They also relate to the principle of dividing the training schedule over a whole year. These ideas are essentially based on the realization that the human organism cannot go beyond its upper performance limit over an extended period of time without a massive collapse of its physical abilities and a loss of psychological performance readiness.

This principle takes into consideration the knowledge (shown graphically as a sine curve) of the development, maintenance, and loss of productivity.

As previously mentioned, the division of a "soccer year" into specific periods reflects the application of that principle:

- Pre-season period (four to six weeks).
- First period of competition (about four months).
- Intermediate period (about two months).
- Second period of competition (about four months).
- Post-season period (about four weeks).

Within each period, the extent and intensity of the stress load (and of the total training program) vary greatly. The graph gives recommendations for structuring the stress load during the actual competitive seasons and the year as a whole.

Aside from the general trend of stress-load training within each period, the total stress load should be reduced every four weeks during the first half of the year and every three weeks over the second half of the year. This allows the biological battery to be recharged and the performance level to be maintained over the long haul.

Total stress load can be reduced by:

- Reducing the extent and, more important, the intensity of the stress load.
- Reducing practice time.
- Reducing the number of training sessions.
- Reducing the specific training methods in favor of overall conditioning exercises.
- Inclusion of alternative athletic activities.
- Increasing other recuperative measures (sauna, massage, etc.).

A yearly plan is created by dividing a long training program into periods of three or four weeks, as discussed on page 24. This kind of planning is helpful in setting objectives for technical and tactical skills.

Interaction of Techniques, Tactics, and Physical Fitness

The basic elements of a player's productivity are his level of technical skills, physical fitness, and tactical skills. All other factors discussed so far, particularly those dealing with training, are important only to the extent that they affect these elements.

It is pointless to ask which of the three elements is the most important for a player's performance. It is part of the uniqueness of soccer that weaknesses in one area can be compensated for by strength in another area. At least this holds true for the beginning and mid-level player. The higher up a player moves, and the stronger the competition, the less likely is it that weaknesses in techniques, tactics, or fitness can be compensated for. That should be no surprise, because techniques, tactics, and fitness are all related, as will be shown in the following discussion.

Influence of Fitness on Techniques

Basic motor skills, power, endurance, speed, and agility are prerequisites for any kind of human movement. The degree to which they are needed depends on the extent, strength, and duration of the movement. This is especially true for the movements of athletes.

Sports-specific techniques also require special fitness-related skills. Here are a few examples:

- Pendulum-like movements of the upper body during a fake require good flexibility and strong muscles.
- A player can execute a flat, hard kick with the arch of the foot only if he has sufficient flexibility (stretching) in his tendons.
- The ability to receive a pass well depends on the suppleness in his hips and on good, overall coordination.
- Effective jumping for heading or quickly confronting an opponent is impossible without well-developed muscles.

In a very important way, a player's technical skills are influenced by his general, as well as

Soccer Training

his specific, endurance level. Once fatigue of the central nervous system sets in, even technically well-coordinated movements won't amount to much.

Influence of Techniques on Fitness

On the other hand, technical skills also influence (particularly over the long haul) the physical condition of a player. Well-coordinated technical movements require comparably less energy and less endurance.

Influence of Techniques and Fitness on Tactics

Successful tactical maneuvering (for definition see page 85) requires clever use of technical skills and physical fitness. This holds true for the tactical skills of individual players, groups of players, and teams. For instance, a tactical maneuver of quick, direct, ball control is doomed when players do not have the necessary, surefooted passing techniques. Modern, tactical variations employed by a team, such as fore-checking (see page 95), require mental alertness and aggressive tackling maneuvers combined with the appropriate techniques. However, exceptional endurance from every player is just as necessary. For the defender, in the last defensive line, additional speed is required. Only when all these requirements are met is it possible to successfully employ these tactics.

As these examples show, one cannot look separately at techniques, tactics, and fitness when examining their impact on winning or losing.

As the performance of Olaf Thon demonstrates, tactical maneuvering (here during a fake) depends to a great degree on the technical skills and physical fitness of the player.

Techniques unique to individual types of athletes are important in different ways. In athletic games such as soccer, a well-polished technique gives a player the chance to solve many game situations.

> Technical training, according to Grosser/Neumaier includes:
> - The ideal model of a movement relevant to a particular sports discipline.
> - The realization of this ideal movement and the most efficient way for a player to carry it out.

Often the ideal movement cannot be carried out because of a player's personal condition (for instance, the stretching ability of the ankle or the ability to angle the foot for kicking the ball). However, the objective in training sessions should always be to reach for the ideal, at least when techniques are practised in isolation.

Considerable deviation from the ideal is often part of athletic activities, and soccer is no exception. Sometimes these deviations are even desired.

Rapidly changing situations during a game often require that the players vary their approach to a technical action and adjust to the situation at hand. For example, a player positioned directly in front of the goal attempts to kick a goal but does not have enough time to carry out the ideal sweeping movement usually prescribed for such a situation. This type of situation has consequences for the training process. On one hand, the player must practise the typical, ideal movement to perfection (with multiple repetitions); on the other hand, he must also have the op-portunity during training to practise an improved technique useful in a real-game situation.

Soccer-Specific Techniques

When we talk about techniques as a solution for athletic tasks, we must ask what task the player has to accomplish in the course of a game.

Fundamentally, we have to distinguish between a task when the player is not in possession of the ball and when he is in possession.

Therefore, we distinguish between:
- Techniques without the ball.
- Techniques with a ball (see overview below).

Receiving and Moving the Ball

How much the technical skills of top professional players have evolved over the last decades can easily be seen when watching their highly developed skills, particularly their running speed when receiving and moving with the ball. In modern soccer, a player must be prepared for interference, and not only by his direct opponent. Because of the tremendous speed players of top teams have, it is not unusual for a player to be challenged by two or even more opponents. Clever ball handling, usually set up by a fake, is one of the most important ways to successfully escape such a situation.

The player receiving the ball combines a body fake and lightning-fast acceleration to rid himself of the opponent(s) (at least for the moment) and to create a new situation.

Implementation
- Receiving a low or high pass from a standing position.
- Moving a low or high pass in the opposite direction from where the ball was played.

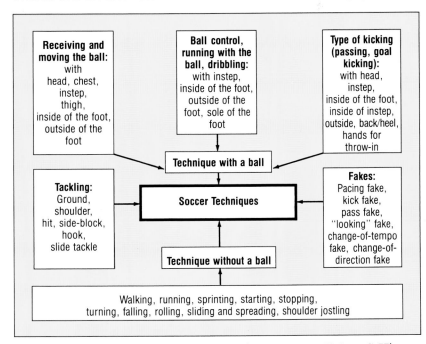

Overview of the technical elements of soccer (see also pages 56 through 57) for goalkeeper techniques)

Techniques and Training

- Moving with the ball after a body fake (right) and the run (to the left) or the reverse.
- Moving with the ball in the same direction from which it was passed (either a low or high pass).

The following is of particular importance for midfielders and forwards: In order to avoid interference from the opposition, a player (who intends to move a pass received in his own territory from a teammate towards the opponents' goal) must be sure to use a body fake to disguise the forward direction of his movement.

Sequence of Movement

Every part of the body (except the hands) can be used for receiving and moving the ball:
- The sole of the foot.
- The inside of the foot.
- The outside of the foot.
- The instep.
- The thigh and shin.
- The stomach.
- The chest.
- The head.

Receiving a ball involves slightly different maneuvers than moving a ball. When receiving, the part of the body that will come in contact is turning towards the ball. The moment the ball makes contact, the body becomes "elastic"—moving with the ball and cushioning its impact. It is important that muscles don't tense up. Moving the ball requires the part of the body that has "received" the ball to refrain from pulling back. Rather, contact must be made in such a way that the ball "stays" in the direction of the movement the player has chosen or the surprise will be lost. This is precisely the reason why muscles should not be

Carrying the ball with the inside of the foot.

1

2

3

tense. In addition, tense muscles don't cushion the impact of the ball.

Mistakes in Moving the Ball

- The "trajectory" of the ball has been misread.
  Correction—Repeated practice of passing from different distances and with different intensity; keeping the eyes on the ball the whole time it is moving.
- The part of the body that will receive the ball has moved "towards" the ball rather than "with" the ball.
  Correction—Move foot, thigh, etc., early enough in the direction of the ball; practise without the ball to get a "feeling" for the movement.
- Muscle groups responsible for the necessary movement are too tense (nervousness, etc.).
  Correction—Consciously practise relaxing, by working with smaller, lighter balls.
- A ball "coming in high" is received with the sole, and the tip of the foot is not lifted up high enough.
  Correction—While standing still, roll a ball back and forth with the sole of the foot.
- A ball "coming in low" is played using the sole, rather than the inside or outside, of the foot.
  Correction—Inform players of the mistake and make the proper reaction "automatic" with frequent practice.

Tips for Training

In the past, it was customary to practise this kind of ball control from a standing position; now it is recommended that players start practising "on the move" early, using exercises and game combinations in which a player learns to "bring the ball along" while run-

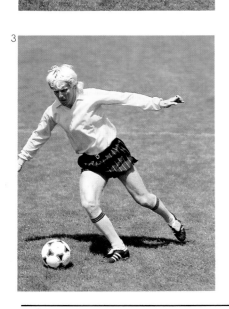

ning. Throughout this practice, the player should be challenged by "opponents." In the beginning, this is on a loose basis, later on it is done more intensively.

Training in Receiving and Moving the Ball Using Mixed Methods

- Alternate practice of handball and soccer with four goals. The ball is thrown in using hands and moved along with the feet, head, and body.
- Instructions, explanations, and demonstrations of ball-receiving and ball-moving techniques.
- Two players run about 30 feet (10 m) apart. Player A passes the ball to Player B, who receives and moves with the ball, practising relevant techniques, including body fakes.
- As above; however, the distance between the two players is increased to 60 to 90 feet (20–30 m), and the ball is passed between them with the instep. At first the ball is thrown by hand; later, it is moved along with the instep.
- One goalkeeper with several groups of paired players. Each of the two-player groups moves within a designated space in half of the playing field. The goalkeeper alternately throws and kicks the ball to one of the two-player groups. Both players of that group start towards the ball and quickly try to establish ball control, drive it, and kick a goal.
- Six-on-six games, using the whole playing field and both goals. Playing under the so-called "provocation rule" (for instance, the ball may not be touched more than three times).

Carrying the ball with the outside of the foot.

Receiving with the chest.

Receiving with the body.

Receiving with the instep.

Techniques and Training

Guiding and Driving the Ball

After receiving and driving the ball, but before a pass or a goal kick, the ball is guided and driven either in various directions or moved with high speed straight ahead. Using fakes, the players have a chance to create new and surprising game situations with individual tactical maneuvers.

Usefulness
- Getting the ball into a different section of the field to shift the game action.
- Driving the ball away from the opposition.
- Controlling the ball to gain time.
- Controlling the ball to give the team a chance to regroup.
- Driving the ball in one direction, and then unexpectedly changing to a new direction.

Sequence of Movements
The sequence of movements when controlling the ball are so varied and numerous that only the very basic principles can be discussed here.

The difference between controlling and driving a ball depends entirely on the dynamics of the sequences of movements. The player usually can run calmly over the playing field, driving the ball with little interference from his opponents, giving him relatively ample time and space.

In an ideal situation, the ball (in a sense) is "glued" to his foot. The player's body is upright, and he is able to keep track of the movements of the opposition as well as those of his teammates. He is looking ahead, approximately 6 to 10 feet (2–3 m) ahead of the ball. This gives him sufficient peripheral vision to see the ball, his

teammates, and the opposition.

The ball can be controlled with the following portions of the foot:
- Inside of the foot.
- Sole of the foot.
- Outside of the foot.
- Instep.
- Heel.

This kind of ball control can be accomplished by using either foot and by using numerous, different combination techniques.

Together with changing directions, doing turns, and rotation maneuvers, the player has a variety of ways to accomplish his task.

Mistakes Made During the Sequence of Movements
- Poor coordination between movements (running, starting, stopping, side to side) and keeping the ball too long. Correction—Pole-running, slalom-style; "fox-hunting" in small groups; running, steadily increasing the speed.
- Driving the ball forward is not carried out with "feeling"—the ball is moving too far ahead of the foot. Correction—As above.
- Driving the ball with the inside, instead of the outside, of the foot or the instep while running fast, resulting in a slower, uneconomical speed. Correction—Running while alternating tempo and driving the ball with the outside or inside of the instep.
- Eyes are fixed too much on the ball and the player does not have enough awareness of what is going on around him. Correction—Shadow-running: Two players, about 50 feet

Moving the ball with the inside, sole, outside, and instep.

(15 m) apart, drive the ball with Player A duplicating the movements of Player B.

Training Tips

Concentrate on using both legs during practice and on moving without fixing the eyes on the ball. According to an established pattern of systematic movements, the ball is driven alternately with the instep, the inside, and outside of both feet. This is followed by using varying techniques appropriate for a given situation, first against one or two opponents, and then by an abbreviated game play.

As soon as a player can use both legs equally well and has a feeling for the size and movements of the ball, he can almost blindly control the ball. He is then able to look around and take advantage of the best passing opportunity. He can also detect the intentions of the opposition, enabling him to take the necessary counter-measures.

It is important that coordination during running and driving the ball be practised with increasing speed. Players will develop assertiveness during competition only if they have practised driving the ball in a staccato-like fashion in all directions.

Examples of dribbling are given in the next section.

Dribbling and Faking

Often the words "dribbling" and "ball control" are used interchangeably. In fact, the basic techniques used to dribble or control a ball are identical. However, in soccer, it has become customary to speak of "dribbling" only when a player, who has ball possession, is being attacked by an opponent. In order to get away from the attacker, the player is forced to camouflage the moves he intends to make. He also has another, additional technique at his disposal: the fake. With the help of a fake, a player can pretend to go in one direction, only to break suddenly (and for the opponent totally unexpectedly) in the opposite direction. By accelerating rapidly, he is able to get safely away from his attacker. Dribbling is one of the most important technical skills a player has, particularly in professional soccer, as has been mentioned before, where a player in possession of the ball is usually pressured by several opponents at the same time.

Through well-coordinated fake movements, a player can shake off his attackers, move to a safer space, or remain in possession of the ball just a bit longer. Dribbling, like no other technique, points up the connection between technical agility and physical fitness. Without agility and flexibility, without enough speed of acceleration, even the most sure-footed player won't be able to extract himself from a tight situation.

Also, the connection between dribbling technique and tactical judgment is very evident. The type and objective of dribbling depends on its tactical possibilities and intentions.

Usefulness

- To break through the defense in the direction of the goal.
- For self-defense, to move in the direction of the midfield in order to gain space.
- To lure the opposition to a particular area in order to make room for passing.
- To take an opponent's attention away from a teammate and then to pass to that teammate.

Sequence of Movements

The different possibilities of controlling a ball have already been discussed on page 40. Combining those different methods creates many different variations for dribbling. It is impossible to list all of them in a book like this. When dribbling, a player will intuitively use the best method, depending on the situation.

Besides the many different combinations of steps involved, variations of dribbling differ most of all in the kind of fakes that a player uses. The most often used are:
- Body and foot fakes.
- Shooting and passing fakes.
- Change-of-tempo fakes.
- "Looking" fakes.

Body and Foot Fake

A player shifting his body or foot position indicates the direction he wants to run. If the opponent reacts and turns to that direction, the player interrupts the initial movement and continues in the opposite direction.

Shooting and Passing Fake

Here, a player pretends that he is about to kick or pass the ball, creating a dangerous situation for the opposition. If the opposition reacts and tries to go after the ball, the dribbler changes his action with a cut movement (if possible with the "wrong" foot) and goes past the opponent(s). The so-called "wrong" foot is the foot the player stands on, to which he has briefly shifted his weight.

Change-of-Direction Fake

Here, a player, running with the ball, suddenly changes direction randomly several times in a row. This maneuver allows him to get past his opponent and to reach the goal.

Techniques and Training

1 **2** **3**

Maneuver with feet without crossing over the ball.

Stopping and starting. The ball is driven with the inside of the foot.

1 **2**

1 **2** **3**

1 **2** **3**

4 5 6

Fake kick and pushing the ball behind the pivot leg.

3 4

Fake stop (with the sole) and driving the ball (called "Leo" or "locomotive").

4 5 6

4 5 6

Techniques and Training

Speed is less important than a good "feel" for the ball.

Faking Change of Tempo

Here, the player slows down and forces the opponent to do the same. At just the right moment, he accelerates very suddenly, leaving the opponent behind. Since the opponent has his back to his own goal, he must first make a 90- or 180-degree turn—one reason why this fake works surprisingly well. In contrast to the direction fake, the tempo is better suited for players with less developed techniques; however, they do need to be good sprinters.

"Looking" Fake

This technique belongs in the repertoire of every top soccer player, although most players at this level are usually so clever that they seldom fall for the trick. Outmaneuvering top opponents requires an atypical, carefully designed fake. One possibility is to pretend to start an action by looking in a particular direction and then suddenly start dribbling for a breakthrough.

Mistakes in the Sequences of Movement

Usually players make the same mistakes discussed in the section on ball control. These mistakes result in the following:

- The fake chosen does not suit the player's style, his technical skills, or his physical condition. Correction—More practice, using different fakes in training games (see above).
- The fake is carried out halfheartedly and without enough confidence. Often a player allows too little time for the fake movements because he does not believe that they will work. However, it is just such a hesita-

tion that renders a fake useless. Correction—Explain to the player the effect of his actions; have him observe a player with good faking skills; have him play defense to see that opponents really do fall for a calm, well-delivered fake.

- The player is not driving the ball hard enough in the new direction and is unable to put enough distance between himself and the opponent. Correction—When faking, position the pivot leg for the next step. Remember that only after the *first step away* from the opponent has dribbling been successful.

Training Tips

On one hand, successful dribbling occurs only when a player has developed a certain feel for ball movement; this comes only with constant practice. On the other hand, dribbling always occurs during the course of a one-on-one confrontation, which requires not only ball sense but also courageous body action. Lightning-fast reactions to an opponent's defensive moves can only be experienced and improved upon in actual one-on-one confrontations. Therefore, constant repetition of the complex sequence of movements involved in dribbling, and the actual experience of these movements during exercise games, are essential.

Methods for Practising Ball Control, Driving, and Dribbling

- Players move with their foot on the ball around randomly arranged poles.
- As the player moves the ball, the coach calls commands indicating how the ball is to be driven,

alternating the inside of the right and left leg with the outside of the left and right leg.
- Players running parallel to each other pass the ball back and forth. The coach runs ahead of them, constantly changing direction from left to right, backwards and forward, to practise "looking" fakes. Players must "mirror" the coach's movements. Speed should increase throughout the exercise.
- Player A (with the ball) runs in front of Player B. A changes direction and tempo suddenly and B must copy A's movements.
- Sprints through randomly arranged stakes and relay races.

Tackling

In the same way that offensive players have to develop a clever way to control the ball and to dribble, defending players have to learn to regain possession of the ball using different techniques.

> Methods of regaining possession of a ball are generally called tackling.

Tackling is only possible when a number of favorable factors are present:

- A player must be motivated, have concentration, be decisive, and be ready to make the risky maneuver confidently.
- A player must be able to recognize the proper moment for tackling. He must not attack too early or too late when attempting to take the ball away from the opponent.
- A player must be in the physical condition specifically required for the tackling techniques (for

instance, good agility in the hips for the hook and the slide tackles).

- A player should be able to anticipate the dribbling action of the opponent.
- Depending on the positions of the dribbler and the opponent, the proper tackling technique must be chosen.
- A player should not have a destructive character, but should be motivated only by his desire to win. After the tackle, he should be able to initiate a new attack. Which tackling technique will have the best chance of success will depend most of all on the position of the two opponents. Do they face each other? Are they next to each other? Behind each other?

The following is a list of different tackling techniques:
- Ground tackle.
- Shoulder tackle.
- Head-on tackle.
- Side tackle.
- Hook tackle.
- Slide tackle.

Ground Tackle

Position of the Two Players
The players are moving directly towards each other. The defending player tackles the opponent who has the ball using his whole body.

Sequence of Movements
The defensive player blocks the ball by applying steady and even pressure with the inside of the leg. All the muscles of that leg are tensed. The tackler should do likewise to protect his knees.

Mistakes
- The defender kicks the ball with the inside of his foot or the instep, instead of blocking the op-

Using a ground tackle, the player blocks the ball with the inside of his foot.

ponent and taking the ball from between his legs. Experience has shown that the ball will move in the direction opposite the tackling player.
Correction—Two-player practise while standing, using reduced power.
Player A hits the ball with the instep; player B blocks it with the inside of his foot.

Head-on Tackle

Position of the Two Players
The tackling player is standing between "man and goal," behind the opponent. In this way, he secures his own goal and has the opponent *and* the goal in his sight.

Sequence of Movements
A tackler, lying in wait, is positioned somewhat diagonally behind the opponent. He starts running with short, quick steps in the direction of the oncoming ball, past the opponent. As soon as the ball is close (both players must be positioned in close proximity), the tackler uses his body to gain a better position from which he can guide the ball (with the inside of

his foot) away from the opponent.

Mistakes
- The defending player is too far behind the opponent, obstructing his own view of the oncoming ball. This position also requires that he first go around the opponent before proceeding forward.
Correction—Constant repetition of one-plus-one-on-one practice in passing, starting, and tackling.

Techniques and Training

1

2

3

Shoulder Tackle

Position of the two players—The players are running next to each other, touching at the shoulders, moving towards the oncoming ball. Both try to gain possession of the ball.

Sequence of Movements

During competition, players can, generally speaking, make contact with an opponent's shoulder, if they keep their elbows close to the body. However, they can do this only when the ball is in close proximity. With a fair, but powerful, use of the body, the player attempts to gain a better position to guide the ball (with the inside of his foot) away from the opponent.

Mistakes

- Making contact with the opponent's shoulder too early and not keeping the elbows close enough to the body are rule violations (pushing).
Correction—Practise shoulder-contact movements without a ball; then with a ball, but with less force.
- Shoulder tackle made at the wrong time (for instance, when the opponent's pivot leg is alongside the player), allowing the opponent to balance himself on the other leg.
Correction—Instruction and practice.

Side Tackle

Position of the two players—The players are alongside each other. The dribbler is in possession of the ball. He tries to kick a pass or a goal.

Sequence of Movements

A tackler runs alongside the opponent (and as close as possible), who is dribbling. When the opponent is about to pass or kick the ball, the player attempts to block the ball with either the inside or the outside of the foot, depending on the order of steps he takes. Here, again, it is important that the muscles be tensed.

1

2

3

4

5

6

Mistakes

- The tackle begins too far away from the dribbling player, creating a kicking angle that lets the ball pass by the tackler's leg. Correction—Encourage the player to make body contact (touching the opponent's shoulder).

Hook Tackle

Position of the Two Players
As with ground tackling, the players face each other.

Sequence of Movements
In low side-tackle position, the

tackler, in a wait-and-see fashion, moves at an angle towards the dribbling opponent. When the opponent lets go of the ball, the player tries to move the ball out of the reach of the opponent.

Mistakes

- The player did not bend down far enough before he attempted the tackle and his body weight shifted too far to one side.

After a shoulder tackle (with elbows close to the body), both players fight for ball possession.

Using a slide tackle, a player shifts his weight after he gets set and pushes off the inside leg, sliding with this leg in the direction of the ball.

4

5

6

Techniques and Training

Examples of Training for the Hook and Slide Tackles

- Stretching exercises (hurdle-jumping body position, leg-splits) to stretch thigh and pelvic muscles.
- At the command of the coach, leg-split exercises while running slowly, alternating between the right and the left leg, followed by body rolling.
- As above, the player is dribbling, and immediately before going into a leg-split the ball is pushed straight ahead about three to six feet (1–2 m).
- Player A slowly moves with the ball; player B runs alongside. When A pushes the ball three to six feet (1–2 m) ahead, B goes after the ball, hooking his leg, and trying to push the ball to the side or trying to block the ball with his body.
- Goal-kicking practice with one-on-one up to six-on-six; passing, however, only after dribbling.

Different Types of Kicking for Passing and Shooting

There are different techniques for kicking the ball. And indeed, kicking techniques are very important in a soccer game. Accurate passes and accurate shots on goal require very specific techniques.

The following lists the different types of kicking:
- Straight-ahead instep kick.
- Inside-the-instep kick.
- Outside-of-the-foot kick.
- Inside-the-foot kick.
- Heading.

As in slide tackling, the player hooks the ball from a low position.

Variations of the Straight-Ahead Instep Kick:
- Hip-pivoting kick.
- Overhead kick.
- Lateral-instep kick.

Whenever a player finds himself in an unfavorable position, or when he wants to surprise the opponent(s) with a pass or kick, he can employ kicks that are not necessarily mentioned in training manuals, such as:
- The back-heel kick.
- Kicking with the tips of the toes.

Whenever strategy requires, the ball can be pushed with the knee. When in the air, it can be pushed or "kicked" with the back of the head. Very important goals have been scored with these rather unorthodox methods, such as Uve Seeler's back-of-the-head kick during the 1970 World Championship Games in Mexico.

The fact that a game situation forces a player to use unusual kicking techniques does not mean that those customarily used are less important. Particularly in professional soccer, a player must be in absolute command of exceptional kicking techniques. Only then will he be able to successfully make tight passes and precise shots on goal, all the while running at top speed over great distances. Mistakes in passing almost always mean loss of ball possession, especially when in his own half of the playing field or in front of his own goal. The opposition will always profit from mistakes of this kind.

For this reason, it is imperative that kicking and passing skills be practised in order to achieve the greatest possible perfection. Fundamental mistakes affecting the sequence of the movements of a ball might go "unpunished" during the early years of play, but they will permanently hinder a player in the development of his performance, and they are almost always impossible to correct. This is why it is so important to correct a beginner's mistakes effectively. Special attention should be paid to this phase in training. With kicking and passing skills, more so than with any other technique, it is essential to recognize the type of mistakes and the reasons for them. The necessary correction depends on what kind of mistake has been made. A coach needs special knowledge in detecting and recognizing these faulty techniques. A discussion of this can be found on page 62.

All kicking techniques have similarly arranged, definite patterns. From a scientific point of view, the training of the sequence of movements is divided into three phases. Each one of these phases has a special function that is indispensable for successfully learning the technique. To correct mistakes, it is equally important to know and understand these phases. The coach must have a clear understanding of the individual actions that involve arms, body, and feet.

The main phases are as follows:

Approach phase—The leg or head moves in the opposite direction of where the ball is to be kicked.

Main phase—The surface of the body meets the ball.

Ending phase—The kicking leg follows through.

Many different kicking techniques are available to a player. Which one is most appropriate for a given situation will depend on the technical perfection a player has achieved. For instance, it is easier to kick with the inside of

the foot than it is with the instep. However, much also depends on which part of the anatomy is used for kicking. For example, a ball can be hit harder and farther with the instep technique than with the technique that uses the inside of the foot. The sequence of the movements (in space and time) are important for a successful kicking technique (successive movements). Also important are the synchronized movements of the pivoting leg, the body, and the arms. These topics are covered in more detail in "Correcting Technical Mistakes" on page 62.

Instep Kick

Kicking straight ahead with the instep is the most powerful kick, and it carries the farthest. It is *the* classic technique for kicking a goal. When the amount of force is carefully measured, it can also be used for short passes. The instep kick technique is better than any other to produce the desired height of a pass, which is controlled by the positioning of the kicking foot. The determining factors are the position of the kicking leg and the pivot leg.

Sequence of Movements

Approach—Straight ahead to the goal.

Pivot leg—Ankle, knee, and hip are lowered.

Free leg—Starting first at hip, then the knee, and finally the ankle joint, it moves back in the approach phase. In the main phase it moves forward towards the ball with a whip-like acceleration from the knee joint. In the ending phase it follows through.

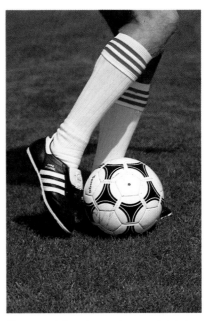

Foot position for an instep kick.

Effectiveness

Passing distance	
too short	xx
Passing distance too long	xxx
Pass too low	xxx
Pass too high	xx
Effective passing	x
Powerful goal kick	xxx
Precision goal kick	xx

Free foot—Flexing the ankle joint, it is supported by tightened muscles.

Kicking surface—The instep.

Upper body—Bent over the pivot leg and the ball.

Techniques and Training

A running, straight-ahead instep kick.

Arms—The arm opposite the free leg moves in step, first back and then forward.

Training Suggestions for Instep Kicking, Simulating Real Game Situation

Mistakes

- Direction of approach and kicking motion not aimed at the goal.
- Pivot leg behind the ball.
- Free leg not bent far enough.
- Free foot not flexed enough.
- Poor kicking surface—instep does not hit the center of the ball.
- Upper body leaning too far back.

- Soccer-tennis in small groups of one-on-one up to three-on-three, with head-high net; depending on the level of skills, receiving the ball or direct passing; "provocation rule," i.e., the ball can only be kicked with the instep.
- "Ball-driving" game with instep technique; using long instep kicks on a narrow section of the field, two groups of players try to push each other out-of-

An inside-the-foot on-the-turn kick, the most demanding variation of the instep kick.

4

5

6

bounds; receiving passes with either foot or hands; throw-in at the point where ball control was regained or where the ball has left the field (on the long side).

- Goal-kicking game using one-on-one: players stand about 30 feet (10 m) away from the goal alternating between playing attacker and goalie; first, the ball is thrown in the air by hand, later drop-kicked, and then played from the ground.
- As above, but distance from the goal increased to 60 feet (20 m), the defender throws the ball 10

feet (3 m) in the air in the direction of the opponent's goal, running after the ball and shooting with the instep.

- As above, but with four players and one ball, the defender has one player passing the ball from the side and a short distance; the oncoming ball is kicked either after one bounce or it is volleyed; later played against opponents.
- Training game with different "provocation rules."

Special Feature of the "Hip-Turn-Kick"

This and the overhead-volley kick are variations of the instep kick. They are intended to allow a high, incoming ball to be played before the opponent can reach the ball.

Sequence of Movements

Pivot leg—Turned towards the goal while kicking the ball.

Free leg—Swings up hip-high in an arch towards the ball.

Upper body—Bending almost horizontally over the pivot leg.

4

5

6

Techniques and Training

The overhead-volley kick, the most spectacular type of instep kick.

Uniqueness of the Overhead-Volley Kick

The overhead-volley kick can be accomplished with or without a scissors movement. With the scissors movement, the player jumps off the kicking leg. The other leg becomes the swinging leg, its action supported by the jump-off leg. The jump-kick leg is forcefully pulled up, past the swinging leg, where it meets the ball at the instep.

Inside-Instep Kick

Even better than the above maneuver is the inside-instep kick, because this technique gives the ball a spin in flight. This phenomenon, known in physics as the "magnus effect," puts a spin on the ball, which creates unequal air pressure around it, moving the ball in an arch-like curve through the air. With the help of this technique, it is possible to score (for instance, using a free kick) by

Foot position for the overhead kick.

Effectiveness

Pass too short	x
Pass too long	xxx
Pass too flat	x
Pass too high	xxx
Pass with spin	xxx
Goal kick too powerful	xx
Goal-kick accuracy	xxx
Direct pass	xx

shooting the ball around the wall, just inside the goal post.

Sequence of Movements

Approach—In an angle in the direction of the goal.
Pivot leg—"Springy" bend at hip, knee, and ankle.
Pivot foot—About two to three feet (1 m) behind the ball.
Free leg—In the approach phase, swings back from the hip and knee, and forward against the ball in the main phase; throughout the main and the ending phase, the leg is rotated at the hip and knee; in the last phase, the leg comes to rest at an angle in front of the pivot leg.
Free foot—Moderately bent at the ankle and rotated to the outside.
Kicking surface—Inside of the instep.

4

5

6

Upper body—Over and in line with the pivot leg.
Arms—Bent at the elbows for balance.

Mistakes

- Approach to the ball too direct.
- Pivot leg too close to the ball.
- Free foot not rotated to the outside. (In all of the cases above, the ball has a strong spin.)
- Free-leg movement from knee joint instead of hip produces weak kick.
- Kicking foot not fixed.
- Upper body leaning too far back.

Outside-Instep Kick

This technique could be called the witches' trick among the kicking techniques, because with this kick a player can solve almost all tactical situations: short, decep-

Effectiveness	
Short pass	xxx
Long pass	xxx
Low pass	xxx
High pass	xx
Passing with spin	xxx
Strong goal kick	xxx
Accurate goal kick	xxx
Direct pass	xxx

tive passes, long passes, kicking with spin, kicking to a teammate who is positioned behind an opponent, even if he seemed to be positively out of reach.

Sequence of Movements

Approach—Straight or slightly angled, depending on the intended spin effect.
Pivot leg—Next to the ball, approximately two feet (1 meter) away.

Pivot foot—"Springy" bend at the ankle, knee, and hip.
Free leg—Swinging straight back from the knee and hip in the approach phase; in the main phase, forward with steadily increasing inside rotation; just before ball contact, increased whip-like action from the knee; decrease of pendulum-like motion and increasing bend at hip and knee.
Free foot—Moderate, inside flex at the ankle in fixed position.
Kicking surface—Outside of instep.
Upper body—Bent forward over the ball.
Arms—Held at the side, bent at elbow for balance.

Mistakes

- Pivot leg too close to the ball.
- Free leg has insufficient swinging motion; rotating motion to the inside.
- Free foot has insufficient inside rotation.
- Upper body leaning too far back.
- Ball hit too close to the center instead of on the side.

The kicking position for outside-instep kick.

Techniques and Training

Inside Kick

This is the most frequently used kick in soccer. The technique allows the player to kick accurately. It is particularly well-suited for combination plays. From a short distance, goal kicking with the inside is more successful than instep kicking. The disadvantage is less power behind the kick; therefore, inside kicks are more suited for short and medium distances.

The kicking position of the foot for the inside kick.

Effectiveness

Long pass	xxx
Short pass	x
Low pass	xxx
High pass	xx
Pass with spin	xx
Strong goal kick	x
Accurate goal kick	xxx
Direct pass	xxx

Sequence of Movements

Anlauf: Geradlinig in Richtung Ziel.
Approach—Straight ahead in the direction of the goal.
Pivot leg—"Springy" bend at the ankle, knee, and hip.
Pivot foot—Next to the ball, one foot-width away from the ball.
Free leg—Swinging back from the hip in the approach phase, forward in the direction of the ball in the main phase, with increasing outside rotation.
Free foot—Rotated to the outside at about a 90-degree angle to the pivot leg; tip of toes pulled up so that the sole is parallel to the ground; ankle fixed by tensing muscles.
Kicking surface—At the inside of the foot at the arch.
Upper body—Leaning over the pivot leg and ball.
Arms—Bent at the elbows and away from the body for balance.

Mistakes

- Toes do not point in the right direction.
- Insufficient outside rotation of the free leg at the hip; insufficiently tensed hip and knee.
- Toes not pulled up sufficiently; ankle not tensed.

- Ball surface is hit too close to the heel or the toes.
- Upper body leaning too far back.

Heading

The heading technique allows a player to reach a high pass, which otherwise could only be played by running backwards. Which player reaches a high-bouncing ball first depends on the timing of the approach.

As in the case with the instep kick, heading techniques also have several variations:

- Header from a standing position—straight ahead.
- Header from a standing position—turning.
- Header from a jump—straight ahead.
- Header from a jump—turning.
- Diving header.

3

4

When heading from a jump, it is best to jump off one leg, since the energy from the momentum of the approach transfers into greater jumping height.

In addition, when heading from a jump and turning, it is best to jump with the leg that is closest to the ball. The other leg, the swinging leg, must not only swing upwards, but in the direction of the ball, increasing the rotation of the hip.

Effectiveness

Short pass	XXX
Long pass	XX
Low pass	
High pass	XXX
Pass with spin	X
Strong pass	XX
Pass accuracy	XXX
Direct pass	XXX

The following discussion refers to headers from a one-leg jump-off without a turn.

Sequence of Movements

Approach—Straight ahead to the ball and the goal; jumping off from the leg that is most appropriate for the situation.

Jump-off leg—Arches backwards after the jump.

Swinging leg—Swinging forward, high up, bending at hip and knee.

Upper body—Arching backwards; the momentum of reaching back in a snapping motion propels the upper body forward; the energy generated puts power behind the header.

Neck and head—Head and neck muscles are tensed by pulling the chin down to the chest during the

A diving header.

upper body's rearward motion; eyes are on the ball.

Kicking surface—The forehead; under no circumstances with the temples.

Mistakes

- Jumping off with both legs instead of one.
- Jump-off leg not arched back immediately; therefore, no counterbalance.
- Too little power behind the swinging motion of the swinging leg.
- Upper body does not reach back far enough.
- Head and neck are not tensed, resulting in neck injuries.
- Eyes are closed.

A jumping header, straight ahead, while running.

4

5

6

7

Techniques and Training

Training Tips for Kicking Methods

Individual kicking techniques discussed in this chapter and the method used for the instep kick point to the importance of kicking practice.

In addition, in the course of training, the following general concepts of kicking are important;

- For ground kicks, the use of *both legs* must be mastered by every player; practising with the weaker leg also strengthens the "good" leg.
- When practising, concentrate first on consistency and precision and then on power.
- Kicking power is less a function of muscle strength than a very well coordinated use of power; therefore, emphasis must be on relaxed, smooth, whipping movements during kicking exercises.
- Long passes and precise shooting require ample space for the free leg and opposite arm during the approach phase.
- Insufficient space is the most frequent reason for mistakes; however, consider these other mistakes: insufficient flexibility in the ankle of the jumping leg (instep kick); insufficient rotation of the ankle (inside kick); insufficient ability for leg-splits (hip-turning kick). Stretching exercises offer the only remedy for these.
- Good timing is a fundamental requirement for converting flanks; a player can only learn the necessary "anticipating" skills by practising, repeatedly, and regularly. PRACTISE! PRACTISE! PRACTISE!
- The training schedule must alternate between different activities: short and long ball practice; balls low and high in the air; straight ahead and from an angle.
- Never start goal-shooting practice without prior, sufficient warm-up, such as shooting from every angle and distance, using every appropriate technique (for instance, from short instances with inside or outside kicks), or without creating complex game situations, shooting and kicking

under time pressure (however, not exclusively). Do not schedule goal-kicking practice for beginners who are tired.

Very Important—Goal kicking livens up every practice session, and, therefore, must be part of the training.

Goalkeeping Techniques

The goalkeeper occupies a special position in soccer. He is allowed to use his hands within the penalty area. Here is a list of techniques specific to this position:

- Fielding low and high incoming balls.
- Fist-punching high balls.
- Deflecting a ball away from the foot of a dribbling opponent.
- Throwing and punting the ball as offensive actions.

Goalkeeping techniques cannot be covered easily in a book dealing with general topics, but they are very important. However, the photos on this and the following page give a good indication of the complexity of the movements involved.

The technique of fielding low passes using the diving method is widely accepted today.

Fielding a ball with the hands.

Catching, fielding, and punting high passes.

A goalie's basic position when catching medium-high passes.

Diving from scissors-step motion, catching, and a soft, two-point landing.

1   2   3

Techniques and Training

Technique Training

The training in techniques occupies a large space within overall soccer training. It should be *the* preparation for competition and, therefore, it should reflect the demands of the "real thing." For this reason, and when time is limited (at least in training programs for young and amateur players), techniques are taught in conjunction with tactical actions and the improvement of physical fitness.

When we talk about technical training, we always talk about the science of movement, teaching a positive change in behavior.

> In this sense, technical training can be defined as: acquiring, improving, stabilizing, and making automatic the varied applications of soccer-specific techniques.

Teaching and Learning Phase

The science of movement includes the above-mentioned level of technical training (acquiring, improving, stabilizing, and making automatic). It also includes the phases of learning motor skills.

However, the development of technical skills, in the strictest sense, does not necessarily happen in a linear, or step-by-step, fashion. This classification should imply that, for instance, players at a particular level acquire techniques which are then refined and stabilized at a later stage.

Rather, the motor skills necessary for sports-specific activities are developed in a spiral fashion (turning a player from beginner

into professional). Each individual spiral represents a different level of performance. On each level, a player must acquire techniques that are then refined, stabilized, and made automatic. Only the quality of these skills is raised from one level to the next. Over time, exercises become more complex, the tempo is increased, and the confrontation between players becomes more intense (see page 61).

Newly acquired techniques must be practised constantly when training young players, long before these techniques have been refined. It does not matter that the skills are not as elegant, are still being acquired, and not automatically available in the beginning. Soccer can be played even if technical skills are still in the infant stage; they only need to be continually improved. A training program for beginners, where practice takes precedence over playing on the field, neither serves to improve technical skills nor to enhance the natural play instinct of the young.

Goals of Technical Training

As indicated above, training objectives must be different for the different levels of age, development, and learning.

Goals for a training program for young people depend on the ages and developmental levels of the players involved. Another criterion is the "training age," which, at the same age level, can differ from one club to another and often even within a club (see page 23).

In a training program for seniors, the goals depend largely on the performance class and, therefore, on the frequency of practice sessions. In lower amateur

classes in soccer, there often is not enough time for practice, making it difficult to develop the talent that is present in the ranks of the players. However, here too, it is important to establish sound training goals and a systematic way to realize them.

Important Points for Technical Training for Young Amateurs

- Continued development of existing individual technical skills. For instance, good heading skills, talent for dribbling, kicking, shooting, etc.
- Correction of obvious technical weaknesses which hinder further development. For instance, poor ball reception, problems due to weak leg(s), weak foot position for instep kicks.
- Scoring goals with head and foot kicks, dribbling from different distances and angles.
- Strengthening the special skills a player needs for his position.
- Development of special techniques for standard procedures, such as corner kicks, free kicks, and penalty kicks.

Important Points for the Technical Training of Professionals

In addition to the goals listed for young and amateur players, the following points are important for professionals:

- Absolute ball control, when running and sprinting.
- Continued development of all techniques to improve strength in one-on-one confrontations, specifically, learning new fakes.
- Continued development of techniques that a player does not necessarily need often in the particular position he holds (developing into an all-around player).

Techniques and Training

Training Principles

The following general principles govern the process of learning and practicing athletic techniques:

- The learning process is successful only if the player has a clear understanding of the motion or movement he is to learn. Therefore, it is essential when teaching beginners to either demonstrate or to show (with the help of photos, or slides) what it is he has to learn.
- Particular techniques require specific physical abilities. If they cannot be acquired in the course of learning a technique, it is necessary to develop them with specific exercises.
- Mistakes in the sequence of movements that have become habitual are corrected only with great difficulty. Therefore, in a training program for beginners, all mistakes must be corrected early on; relearning is very time-consuming;
- Whenever physical abilities have improved (for instance, sprinting), it is necessary to adapt the technical abilities to the new level of performance.
- Children learn new techniques quickly, but they also forget quickly. This makes it necessary to include constant repetition of newly acquired skills in the training program.
- Fatigue interferes with coordination. It is difficult to learn new movements when tired. There-fore, new techniques should be taught at the beginning of a session, immediately after the warm-up.

Specific Principles

- Professional players must be able to perform techniques with both legs. Therefore, from the very beginning, practice with both legs should be included in training.
- Techniques should be performed "heads-up." Keeping an eye on the ball must become automatic.
- Techniques should be practised with a gradual increase in tempo. Quick leg work while standing and while running must be a constant part of the training program.

Children react to technical training with enthusiasm. Playing ball is fun!

Techniques and Training

Methods, Exercises, and Games for Technical Training

Technical training consists of two different types of training:
1. Game plays allow a player to acquire, stabilize, and make automatic ball-control skills (inductive learning)
2. Exercise helps a player consciously learn to use the individual elements of the technique (deductive learning).

Learning takes place by two entirely different methods:
1. Learning of individual elements by themselves.
2. Learning several technical elements within complex actions.

Consequently, a coach can choose between the following:
- Game method.
- Individual exercises.
- Complex exercises.
- Combinations of two or more of the above.

The Game Method

The game method teaches complex playing skills using real game situations and different types of strategies. This teaches technical skills automatically.

Here, teaching takes place through the play method, which is known in sports didactics as the "holistic method." This teaching method is less "teacher intensive" than that organized around an exercise session. The assumption is that, in the course of a game, a player learns technical and tactical skills through experience (inductive teaching method), and the player also learns and improves his skills automatically.

Examples of Game Plays

There is a great variety of small game plays that lead to the "big game." The following is a selection of some of the typical methods.

Game Without a Goal and with Unrestricted Space
- Competition (one-on-one up to eight-on-eight) with different tasks. For instance, controlling the ball within a group; passing the ball from player A to player B to player C, etc.; combination play with double pass; plays with one or two ball-contacts per player; playing using only the right or left leg for passing; passing only after one dribble; etc.
- Catch-ball with two-on-one, three-on-one, four-on-two, six-on-two.
- Game in which one team outnumbers the other team.

Games with a Goal, Within Lines, or Random Goals
- Goal-shooting games, goal-scoring competitions between two or four players, respectively, from about 30 to 60 feet (10–20 m).
- Game plays with one-on-one up to eight-on-eight with two, four, or six small goals.
- The same between two touch-lines. Here one goal or point is scored whenever a player dribbles across the opponent's line.
- Game plays with neutral players throwing the ball in. For example, one neutral player for both five-on-fives. Passes caught by the neutral players count as a score or point.
- Soccer-tennis games. The height of the net and the size of the playing field determine the degree of difficulty.

Small, competitive games, called *circular group games*, have been developed by Brüggemann/Albrecht. The game ideas, development, and organization are presented with three different types of rules.

The game "one and two-on-two with a goal," for example, is played on the regular field with the penalty area extended to midfield. The rules are as follows:
1. The *provocation rule*—Goals can only be scored by dribbling or by trying to pass from outside of the penalty zone. This rule "provokes" players to use very specific technical-tactical skills.
2. The *continuation rule*—After gaining ball possession, the player must first pass the ball back to a neutral player positioned in the center circle before the team in possession of the ball is allowed a goal kick.
3. The *correction rule*—Goals attempted from the outside of the penalty area can only be made by a direct kick after a back pass.

Simple Exercise Method

The "simple-exercise method" is traditionally used as a special form of the "partial method."

This method allows technical and tactical elements (important for a player's total game performance) to be practised in isolation with many repetitions.

This method of teaching, consisting of simple exercises, is very teacher-intensive (deductive learning method). Here, "simple" means that the actions are not yet part of complex game strategies, and players are not yet getting sidetracked into more complex actions. Soccer training today makes increasing use of practising only one part of the overall game action, such as the hip-turn kick. This method is particularly useful for teaching or strengthening new techniques when there is little time available for training.

It must be clearly stated that a soccer training program with too much emphasis on this method is not considered to be up-to-date. This is especially true for training beginners.

Exercise Games

- Individual exercises with the ball to improve "feeling" for the ball, such as dribbling, running a slalom course, running in a designated circle; ball-control practice alternating the inside and outside of the foot and alternating the left and right foot.
- Exercises in groups of two to six players, standing and running.
- Heading exercises on the wall.
- Running relay races.

- Combination plays in groups of two or three players using a pre-arranged running route. A continuous increase in difficulty is achieved by using three different kinds of exercises, such as:
- a. Exercises while standing (hardly used today).
  b. Running exercises (jogging, running, sprinting).
  c. Exercises against an opponent (an imagined opponent, a half-active opponent, and then an active opponent).

For children, one-on-one exercises have all the elements of a game.

Complex Exercises

Here, specific plays are taken from real-game situations and practised through constant repetition.

Techniques and tactics are used as they would be in a real game. Repetition is the teaching tool. The goal and the effectiveness of the method make this the intermediate step between simple exercises and the game-play method.

Examples of Exercises

- Starting from the sides at midfield, a left- or right-winger and a center forward, opposed by one or two players, drive the ball in the direction of the goal line, concluding the exercise with a pass to a center forward.
- While running, a forward passes to a center forward. This player then passes to a third player in midfield (either by kicking or using a header) who has moved up, and who attempts a shot on goal from the second line. Both forwards may be pressured by players from the opposition.

The **degree of difficulty** of this method can be increased by the following, systematically employed steps:
- Exercises according to specific game strategies with "half-active" opponents.
- Exercises according to varied game strategies that are used with "half-active" opponents.
- Solving game situations using all techniques practised so far.

Basically, the number of opponents can be increased so that the offense is outnumbered by the defense, both sides have an equal number of players, and the offense outnumbers the defense.

Techniques and Training

Advantages and Disadvantages of the Methods

Discussions about the advantages and disadvantages of the methods listed here have been (and still are) numerous. Each one of the three methods has specific advantages and disadvantages. However, they all have their place in a modern training program. In fact, it is difficult to imagine a program without them. Which method to use depends on the following:

- The goal set for daily training.
- How much time is available for training.
- How many balls and how much equipment is on hand.
- The age and the developmental level of the players.
- Training readiness.
- The performance level of the players.

On pages 60 and 61, we discussed the applications, advantages, and disadvantages of the different methods. Depending on the specific training situation, a coach may want to put more emphasis on one method than on the others.

For instance, in schools today, the game-play method is often used exclusively, since experts believe that the overriding objectives (such as socialization and affective learning), or process-oriented teaching, are easier to accomplish this way than they would be by using methods that train skills in isolation.

If time is limited, and a coach needs to address a specific technique, isolated exercises are the best choice.

For more advanced young players and for senior players, the complex method is particularly useful, because all performance-related aspects are being trained as close to the real situation as possible. When training junior players, it is best to alternate between playing, exercising, and playing again.

Mixed Method

When contrasting all three training methods, it is clear that no one method alone is ideal for all situations. Basically, using a mix of all three methods in the course of an individual training session (especially when used during several, consecutive sessions) will have the greatest benefit. As far as the concept of the "whole-part-whole" method is concerned, the ideal solution during a training session is to alternate between game plays, exercise, and game plays. In this way, the advantages of each method are maximized, and the disadvantages are minimized.

The first step is for a player to learn the importance of individual techniques while playing a game. This serves as motivation for the second step: the separate training of individual elements. The effectiveness (and with that the **meaning of training**) becomes clear when a player can check his skills in a game-play situation within the same training session and realize how much his skills have improved.

Correcting Technical Mistakes

In the course of the training program, a player will automatically make mistakes in the sequence of movements. If these mistakes are not recognized and corrected immediately, they will become ingrained, which is a great disadvantage for the development of the player. Even later, when a player has already learned the basics, mistakes appear that have to be corrected.

Sadly, too many coaches still don't have a good eye for or the necessary skill to recognize the reasons for the mistakes. Thus, they do not intervene with systematic and proper exercises.

Techniques are inadequate when the sequence of movements deviates significantly from the ideal for the following criteria:

- Improper spatial position and timing of simultaneous and consecutive movements of arms, legs, upper body, and head. (Compare discussion of the Sequence of Movements under "Kicking.")
- Energy not used economically (often found with nervous players).
- Poorly coordinated movements.
- Strength, tempo, and the extent of motions are not appropriate for a particular movement.
- The sequence of movements is not sufficiently consistent and precise.

A coach needs a great deal of experience to recognize the many possibilities for mistakes. He must be as committed to gaining this experience as he expects his players to be in learning how to avoid the mistakes.

Reasons for Mistakes

There are as many reasons for the mistakes as there are reasons for faulty movements. It is true that a player might not be very talented and that the training time has not been sufficient to gain the necessary technical perfection. There are a number of other possible reasons, such as:

- Insufficient motivation as well as the factors that affect it: concen-

tration and attentiveness.
- Not clearly understanding (or even totally misunderstanding) the sequence of movements.
- General or specific physical shortcomings.
- Wrong teaching methods or demands raised too quickly.
- Fear of injuries or failure.
- Insufficiently healed injuries interfering with performance.
- Poorly developed "feeling for movement" (the body's periphery gives faulty feedback to the central nervous system and the player perceives movements differently from the way they are actually carried out).
- Transferring movements from other sports (for instance, the use of both feet when heading, as in volleyball), leading to inap-propriate movements.

The number of possible mistakes and the reasons for them increases the difficulty in finding the proper corrections.

Additionally, although mistakes may seem visually identical, the reasons for them might be different. For instance, a player's weak heading skills might be the result of insufficient jumping power or of a fear of injury.

Corrective Measures

Corrective measures must be carefully chosen to address the specific reason for a faulty movement. Depending on the reasons, the following corrections are recommended:
- Repeated demonstrations and explanation of the *proper* movement.

If technique is still faulty:
- Demonstration and explanation of the *wrong* movement, so that the player becomes conscious of his mistake.
- Simplifying exercise and game methods.
- Assigning specific tasks. For instance, kick only low passes. This is an instep-kick exercise that leads to better foot and upper-body positioning.
- Actively guiding the body into the proper position. The coach keeps the player's upper body straight during a hip-turning kick.
- Reducing fear through exercises and game playing with a lighter ball (for instance, during heading practice).

Physical Fitness and Fitness Training

In the sense of its Latin meaning, *"conditio sine qua non,"* fitness is the "requirement, without which nothing will work." In sports, fitness is a buzz word for many different abilities and qualities that are fundamental for any type of athletic performance. The connection between techniques, tactics, and physical fitness has already been discussed on page 35. As was stated, physical skills and, specifically, the actual availability of them during competition depends on many different factors.

Factors of Physical Conditioning

In the literature, there are two different definitions, or descriptions, for the concept of "conditioning."

In a broader sense, conditioning refers to the physical and psychological quality necessary for athletic performance (see the table on page 17). These rather different qualities and skills are constantly interacting with one another and are mutually dependent on each other during athletic activities. For example, when dribbling or shooting a goal, the effect of the necessary power is influenced and guided by psychological factors, such as motivation and concentra-

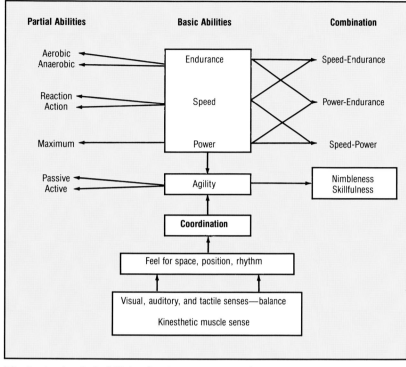

The basic physical abilities (in the narrow sense), their different components, their functional connection, and the types of combinations resulting from those abilities.

tion. Every coach knows that even though his team seems to be in top physical condition, nervousness and fear can interfere with the ability to perform well.

In a narrower sense, fitness in sports and in training refers to motor skills, power, endurance, speed, agility, and coordination.

In sports-science literature, the factors of fitness, such as power, speed, and agility, are also defined as motor activities of the muscular system, requiring physical conditioning and physical skills.

Even if the best description of the general concept is the interconnectedness of the process, the following observation is made from the second, narrower interpretation.

The specific condition of a soccer player is a combination of power *and* endurance, power *and* agility, power *and* speed. (See table).

Factors Influencing Physical Conditioning

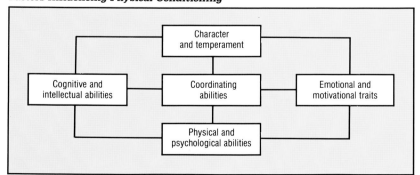

Physical Fitness and Fitness Training

Power and Power Training

> In sports, power is defined as the ability to overcome or counteract resistance through muscle activity.

Resistance in this sense is that gravity and inertia of a player's body that the player must overcome.

The muscular system does its work in different ways through different forms of contractions. We differentiate between three types:
- Dynamic accelerating (jumping).
- Dynamic bending (landing).
- Static holding and moving (for instance, during one-on-one confrontations).

These are activated by different types of muscle contractions.

A Slight Diversion

The Muscle System

The human body has three different kinds of muscles:
- Smooth muscles (of the inner organs) are controlled by the autonomic nervous system.
- The cardiac, or heart, muscle has its own control system.
- Skeletal muscles are controlled by the central nervous system, as has already been mentioned.

Depending on the structure and function of the skeletal muscles, we distinguish between two main types:
- The white, fast muscle fibre (fast twitch = f.t. fibre), which is primarily involved in quick, power-intensive movements.
- The brown, slow muscle fibre (slow twitch = s.t. fibre), which is active during muscle activities of less intensity, but for longer duration.

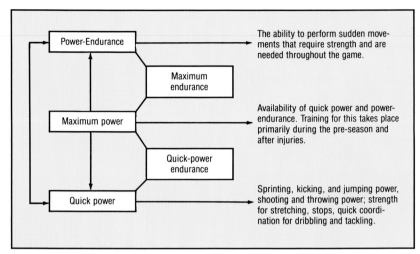

The basic motor skills of power and strength, sub-skills, and their importance for the performance skills of a player.

Quality of Power-Strength

Depending on the degree of the resistance the muscular system must overcome, the length of time that the system is able to do so, and the speed with which muscles contract while dealing with the resistance, we talk about different qualities of muscle power-strength (see the table above).

These power-strength qualities are not all equally important for soccer players. Since the physiology of muscles and the process of nerve impulses differ, it is necessary to choose the proper training method for the development of power-strength.

Maximum Power-Strength

> Maximum power-strength represents the highest level of power a player can generate through his own willpower.

This quality depends on the type of muscle fibre an individual has and on the inter-muscle coordination. The thicker the individual muscle fibre is, and the better a muscle has been trained to contract (at the same time, as many individual fibres as possible), the greater the maximum power-strength.

The output of the muscle can by dynamic as well as static. Accordingly, training can consist of isometric, as well as isotonic, muscle contractions (isotonic or isometric training, respectively).

> Note: Sufficient maximum power-strength is the prerequisite for optimal development of quick power and power-strength endurance.

Quick Power

> Quick power is the ability of the muscular system to overcome resistance by quick contractions of the muscle fibres.

The level of this ability can be a limiting factor in the performance of a player. The extent to which quick power can be generated is also influenced by the amount of maximum power-strength. This has consequences for the training of quick power.

Power-Energy Endurance

> This is the ability to sustain powerful movements or actions over an extended period of time without experiencing obvious fatigue.

During game plays, continuous power-strength performances are kept at a low to moderate level. This develops sustained power-energy endurance.

Aerobic endurance is important for this power-energy quality (see page 75) because of the fast re-synthesizing process of phosphate, the energy-producing mineral.

The Significance for the Player

Without a sufficient level of power-energy in the leg and body muscles, a player cannot satisfy the high demands of a dynamic sport. Without a well-developed capacity for power-energy he will be highly susceptible to injuries. A player needs quick power-energy to be able to accomplish fast starts and stops, and for dribbling, tackling, shooting goals, and heading. He also needs it in different forms, such as shooting power and jumping power.

A player needs maximum power-energy of the stretching muscles of the legs and the body as a basis for quick power-energy. This is the best insurance against injuries during quick, powerful movements.

Vaulting.

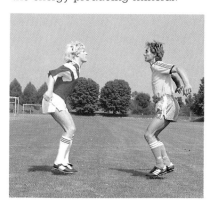

Chest bouncing.

Shoulder tackling while jumping.

Pulling against resistance.

Alternating rolling and jumping.

Physical Fitness and Fitness Training

It is hoped that fitness clubs, which are appearing all over the place, reduce the aversion against such exercises, and increase participation through the opportunities they offer.

In soccer training, maximum power-energy is usually being created during the preseason, between seasons, and after injuries. For rehabilitation after injuries—in addition to physical therapy—isometric exercises and exercises on isokinetic power equipment are remarkably effective. One-sided muscle deficits can be successfully treated with those exercises, and the danger of a player reinjuring himself can be avoided.

Power Training

Power training should follow a sufficient warm-up. Muscles must be allowed to stretch and loosen up between exercises. The individual power-energy training is as follows:

Maximum Power Training

First Phase—Muscle-Development Training

This training increases the size of all white muscle fibres.

Training Method:	
Extensive Interval Training	
Intensity	50–70%
Series	3–5
Repetitions	many
Length of breaks	1–2 minutes
Tempo	slow to medium

Second Phase—Coordination Training

Here, the muscle learns to voluntarily contract as many fibres as possible at the same time. The muscles of a well-trained athlete

contract up to 85 percent of the muscle fibre at the same time. The inter-muscular coordination of a less athletically inclined person is clearly much weaker.

Training Method:	
Intensive Interval Training	
Intensity	75–100%
Series	5–8
Repetitions	3
Length of breaks	2 minutes
Tempo	quick

For most of the exercises, the player's own body weight is sufficient for maximum power training. Additional weights, such as a sandbag or medicine ball do not increase the training effect appreciably.

Types of Training

- Intensive exercises on weight equipment (leg presses, etc.) for the muscle groups that move ankle, knee, and body.
- Knee bends with dumbbells (bending up to 60 degrees).
- Exercises with a partner on the back (climbing stairs, etc.).
- Jumping off steps, the edge of a box, or a low table and immediately jumping up (high jump) after the landing (polymetric training); also, with weights (using a weight vest or sandbag for additional weight), trying to reach the greatest possible height when jumping.
- Brisk bending and stretching of one leg (also done with added weights).

Quick-Power Training

For a boost in maximum power during the season (after deliberate training during the pre-season), players do not need to do general training exercises without a ball. Except for the active season,

quick-power training can be incorporated in exercises geared towards the overall development of the players (see below). Game-specific training (such as game plays in small groups) gives ample impetus for the improvement of intra- and inter-muscular coordination, covering special quick-power needs at the same time.

Training Method

Exercises for Overall Development

- All soccer-specific game plays: one-on-one up to eight-on-eight.
- All running and rough-and-tumble games.
- All running and jumping exercises where the body's own weight is used for quick-power movements (jumping up and down, jumping and running forward, jumping or running uphill (or stairs), zigzag jumping (jumping on one leg).
- All exercises involving pushing and kicking the ball with the forehead; exercises with a suspended ball.
- Push-pull exercises with a partner.
- Hurdle jumping over several partners.

Specific Exercises for the Body

- Rigorously played rough-and-tumble games.
- Sit-ups from a reclining position on the floor or on a slanted board.
- Stretched out on the floor, using the abdominal muscles to simultaneously lift the legs and the upper body.
- Throwing exercises with a medicine ball.
- Exercises with a partner involving lifting, carrying, pushing, and pulling.

Physical Fitness and Fitness Training

Strengthening the knee bends.

Leg lifts to strengthen stomach muscles.

Knee stretches.

Lifting the upper body to strengthen stomach muscles.

Pushing legs under and over a rope in quick succession to strengthen stomach muscles.

Lateral push-ups to strengthen muscles.

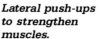

Physical Fitness and Fitness Training

Power-Energy Endurance Training

Essentially, endurance is a function of maximum power and aerobic stamina. It is not necessary to do separate power-energy endurance training when occasional training sessions for maximum power and soccer-specific endurance training are scheduled.

If, however, maximum training is not scheduled at least every three weeks, the following training methods should be included in the regular training session.

Training Methods

The same extensive interval method can be used that was recommended for power-endurance training. Specially organized circle games are very effective.

Types of Training

Most of the exercises listed under training for maximum power and quick power can also be used here. In comparison to the quick-power training, load intensity is somewhat reduced (i.e., using a lighter medicine ball), and the duration of the load is increased. The tempo should not be reduced, since that would have a negative effect on the quick-power performance.

Additional Exercises

- Running 150–300 feet (50–100 m) in relay races or carrying a partner on the back.
- Same exercise, but two or three players carry one (Roman chariot race).
- Four-on-four "horseman-soccer" using a small-size goal. Each team consists of two players—one is the rider; the other is the horse. Duration of play is two minutes; after two minutes, the players change positions.

- Medicine ball with a heavy strap (or in a net with a long strap) is swung with both arms around the body; upper body moves in a wide circle (see photo page 80).

Speed and Speed Training

The speed of a soccer player is much more complex than, for instance, the speed of an athlete running the 100-meter dash.

Speed in soccer is a combination of several single skills that can best be defined as:

1. The ability to recognize a game situation and its possibilities as quickly as possible = **speed of recognition**.
2. The ability to anticipate the development in a game situation, particularly the behavior of the opponent directly involved, as quickly as possible = **speed of anticipation**.
3. The ability to react quickly to unforeseen situations during the game = **reaction speed**.
4. The ability to rapidly change direction when running fast without a ball = **speed of changing directions**.
5. The ability to carry out game-specific actions with the ball under time pressure = **action speed**.

Implications for the Player

The qualities listed above are of paramount importance for today's soccer player. All phases of mod-

ern soccer have become much more dynamic, more athletic, and faster. A player can only do justice to these developments if his thought processes, reactions, and actions are flexible and quick. The table on the opposite page compares the different qualities of speed with a few typical game situations in which they would be used.

Speed of Recognition

A player is constantly bombarded with numerous visual and auditory stimuli. He must choose those that are relevant to a given game situation. Instant recognition requires the following:
- High motivation.
- Years of experience.
- Freedom from fear and stress.
- A combination of general and specific attentiveness.

Speed of Anticipation

The ability to anticipate developing game actions is closely tied to the experience a player has had. Older players (i.e., the sweeper), with superior speed-of-anticipation, are able to compete successfully with younger players, even though younger players can react faster.

Speed of Reaction

Whenever a goalkeeper has to react to a sudden shot on goal, or a defender to an opponent's dribbling action, anticipation plays only a secondary role. In such cases, the speed of reaction is the deciding factor.

Reaction time is the time it takes for a stimulus (for instance, the kick of the ball towards the goal) to translate into the first visible reaction of the muscular system. Reaction time depends on:
- The type of stimulus (auditory,

Physical Fitness and Fitness Training

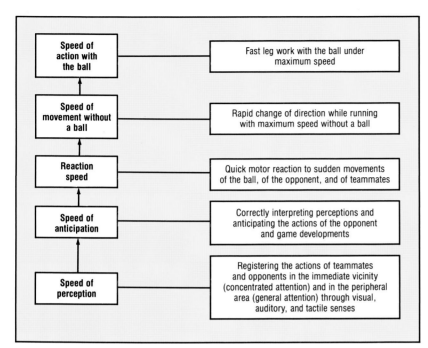

Speed of action with the ball	Fast leg work with the ball under maximum speed
Speed of movement without a ball	Rapid change of direction while running with maximum speed without a ball
Reaction speed	Quick motor reaction to sudden movements of the ball, of the opponent, and of teammates
Speed of anticipation	Correctly interpreting perceptions and anticipating the actions of the opponent and game developments
Speed of perception	Registering the actions of teammates and opponents in the immediate vicinity (concentrated attention) and in the peripheral area (general attention) through visual, auditory, and tactile senses

Characteristics influencing speed, and their importance for the performance level of a player.

visual, or tactile). A player must react rapidly to visual stimuli; for that reason, the coach should not use a whistle when practising reaction speed.

- The type of reaction necessary (simple reaction, chosen from several possible stimuli, and reaction to complex stimuli).
- Choosing an action depends on the level of skills and the experience of the player.

Speed of Direction Change (without the ball)

Here, the initial speed and the acceleration are most important. A player's progress is often interrupted by stops and change of directions, as he adjusts to the actions of the opponents. This kind of speed is influenced by the following factors:

- The ability of the leg muscles to stretch instantly and powerfully, which in turn is based on maximum-power availability.

- Quick, well-coordinated leg and foot work.
- All-around, good coordination.
- Skills to coordinate actions automatically.

Action Speed (with the ball)

Winning a game always depends on the speed with which players receive and drive the ball, keep possession of the ball under pressure from the opponent while running at high speed, driving and dribbling ability, and how well they can make accurate shots on goal.

Even though these skills are built on speed without a ball, they are intimately related to the ball sense and technical skills a player possesses. Many players are simply "too fast" for systematic game strategies. They have yet to match their technical skills to their innate speed skills.

The training of game-specific action speed is, most of all, de-

signed to achieve optimum coordination between speed of movement and technical motor action. This is accomplished by combining high-speed running during techniques and tactics exercises with games using "provocation rules."

Speed Training

Most of the qualities that make a player "fast" are game-specific. Therefore, training is only successful when using game plays and exercises with a ball. However, the power of leg and body muscles often limits acceleration speed, and, likewise, good acceleration skills interfere with fast foot work. For that reason (at least for performance-oriented soccer training), it is necessary to add systematic sprint training with the ball to the training that develops power-energy.

The following general, as well as soccer-specific, principles have to be taken into consideration.

General Principles

- Speed training without intensive warm-up is poison. It produces injuries.
- Speed training is useless when a player is tired. At best, it increases speed-endurance; usually, it decreases speed.
- Training intensity must be kept to a maximum or high level; otherwise, it only benefits endurance and does not increase speed. This is particularly important when breaks are short.
- The training must be short, and the intensity low. When running 100–150 foot (30–50 m) sprints, breaks should be at least three minutes long. They can be used for light exercises with a ball or

Physical Fitness and Fitness Training

for relaxation and stretching exercises.

- Moderate sprints in slightly hilly terrain are good for improving foot work (developmentally at its peak between the ages of 13 and 15).
- Sprinting in moderately elevated terrain with additional weights is recommended to improve speed-power.

Factors influencing speed are different and can be adjusted to each developmental stage (sensitive phase). Results will vary. For instance, foot work can be improved successfully between the ages of five and seven. Also, reaction speed can be improved considerably around the age of 10, but less so when a player is six or seven years old. Muscle mass, however, will not increase until puberty.

Specific Training Principles

- Speed of perception depends to a great degree on psychological factors. In part these factors are influenced by heredity, but they can also be positively influenced by a systematic training approach (i.e., by creating an optimum level of motivation, reduction of fear, etc.).
- During competition, a player is constantly challenged to choose among several visual stimuli; for this reason, it makes sense to conduct game-specific reaction-speed training in the form of small game plays.
- General and specific speed coordination can be improved by playing rough-and-tumble games.

Types of Training

- All suitable game plays with relevant game rules.
- All technical training under

high and maximum tempo.

- All forms of exercises that improve maximum power and speed-power of leg and body muscles.
- Sprints with and without a ball over 15 to 100 feet (5–30 m) and from different positions (standing, laying flat on the back, or on the stomach); additional exercises can be included in these sprints, such as half turns of the body, full turns, simulated head kicks, fakes, etc.

This competitive scene clearly shows how much speed the game of soccer demands from the players.

72

Physical Fitness and Fitness Training

In general, sprints should not go beyond 100 feet (30 m); ideal are:

- Sprints of 15 feet (5 m) and 50 feet (16 m).
- Slalom runs where the distance between poles is 5 to 30 feet (2–10 m).
- Relay competitions.
- Running and rough-and-tumble games.
- In groups of two, shadow games with changing speeds.
- Relaxed running with increasing and varying speeds.

Endurance and Endurance Training

Soccer games played according to international rules have two 45-minute periods. Top players will cover a distance of up to nine miles (14 km) (see table, page 76). These two facts alone show how important endurance is for the effectiveness of a soccer player.

> In athletics, endurance is defined as the physical and psychological strength to overcome fatigue due to prolonged, intense activities and the ability to recover rapidly.

Endurance for training purposes, as far as motor activities are concerned, has further subdivisions. One is a division into time periods:

- Short-term endurance—45 to 120 seconds.
- Medium-term endurance—2 to 8 minutes.
- Long-term endurance—over 8 minutes.

Long-term endurance is further divided (see page 74), taking into account different requirements in energy availability:

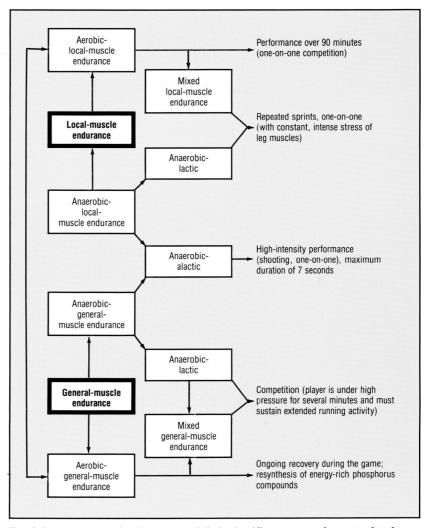

Partial components of endurance and their significance to performance levels.

- Long-term endurance I—up to 30 minutes.
- Long-term endurance II—30 to 90 minutes.
- Long-term endurance III—over 90 minutes.

Because of the involvement of different parts of the muscular system, we distinguish between:

- Individual or local muscle endurance.
- General muscle endurance.

Approximately one-sixth to one-seventh of the total muscle mass is involved; together, the muscles of both legs make up about one-sixth of the total muscle mass.

Depending on the type of energy required, we distinguish between:

- Aerobic endurance.
- Anaerobic endurance.
- General or mixed aerobic endurance.

Depending on the work that muscles perform, there is a further division:

- Dynamic endurance.
- Static endurance.

The complexity of the connection between the individual types of endurance can be seen in the table above.

Physical Fitness and Fitness Training

From the many partial components of the different types of endurance only a few are important for soccer.

Importance for the Player

The distances and intensities of running required in professional soccer are listed in the table on page 76. A player (depending on his position and the performance class) covers about 10 miles (14 km)) in the course of one game. He runs in relatively short (1–10 second) bursts, followed by longer "breaks." While walking and/or jogging, lactic acid, which accumulates over time, is, to a great extent, broken down by the aerobic process.

According to Linsen (1983), during the course of a game the average accumulation of lactic acid is approximately 4 to 7 mMol per quart of blood. This is low when compared to intensive training of anaerobic medium-period endurance (for which 20 mMol per quart of blood has been measured). Given the results of these measurements, it can be stated that a soccer player in top condition needs the following, specific endurance capabilities:

- General endurance, because he uses one-sixth of the total muscle mass during running.
- Dynamic endurance, because only dynamic muscle activity takes place during a game.
- Extremely rapid short-term endurance with maximum power-energy output and speed, up to 10 seconds.
- Aerobic long-term endurance, based on a well-functioning, physiological process where glycogen, and to some extent fat, are broken down.

Also needed, although to a

Type of Energy-rich Substances in Muscle Fibres and Their Importance for Athletic Performance (compiled from information supplied by Weineck, 1988)

	Availability in the body in large calories (Kcal)	Maximum time	Rate of movement: possible speed of muscle contraction	Comment
Adenosine triphosphate (ATP)	1.2	0–2 seconds	approximately 100%	only sufficient for 2–3 muscle contractions
Phosphocreatine acid	3.6	2–20 seconds	approximately 90%	up to 7 seconds, exclusively responsible for ATP resynthesis
Breakdown of glucose	1,200	7–10 seconds	approximately 50%	after 7 seconds' lactic-acid buildup, reaching maximum buildup at 40–70 seconds
Anaerobic glucose breakdown	5,024	7–10 seconds	approximately 25%	for soccer players, very important for the resynthesis of ATP
Aerobic breakdown of fat	50,000–209,340	60 seconds up to several hours	approximately 12%	delivers approximately 30% energy during rest

much lesser extent, is anaerobic endurance. Long-term anaerobic endurance capability is important because it is responsible for the process that makes energy available by resynthesizing energy-rich phosphorus compounds.

As an Aside

In professional soccer during the 70's, the anaerobic short- and medium-term endurance training was much favored. The interval method, using repeated running exercises with and without a ball, was a particular favorite during the pre-season and in the middle of the season. This highly intensive training method created considerable stress due to the repetition of training stimuli. The result of constant stress is an increase in lactic-acid buildup,

followed by impaired coordination and the loss of important vitamins (B, C, E) and minerals (calcium, potassium, and magnesium), causing enzyme functioning to be disturbed for many days.

Today, we know that these training methods do not contribute to an improvement of soccer-specific endurance; rather, they decrease the existing aerobic endurance.

Highly intensive interval training should only occasionally be included in the training program (approximately every 14 days) during the competitive season.

Factors Influencing Aerobic, Long-Term Endurance

A host of different requirements have to be met before aerobic

Physical Fitness and Fitness Training

endurance is achieved. Some of these factors are:

- Sufficient level of glycogen. Glycogen is stored directly in the fibre of the muscle and in the liver. Training can increase the amount of glycogen stored in the liver.
- Sufficient level of enzyme activity, which guides the breakdown of glycogen and fat. These enzyme activities are also positively influenced during training.
- Improvement of the cardiovascular system (increasing the size of the heart muscle and the number of capillary blood vessels in the muscles). Endurance training almost doubles the oxygen-exchange surface.
- Sufficient amount of blood for the transportation of oxygen, and as a means of dealing with the increased acidity. The number of red blood cells also plays a roll in this process.
- Improvement of the intake and use of oxygen. The latter, in particular, is positively influenced by training.

Endurance Training

Depending on the type used, endurance training can create very different levels of stress for a player. The overall stress load players are exposed to can be controlled by the choice of methods and objectives that a coach establishes when putting together the yearly training schedule. Proper choices, therefore, are a basic prerequisite for the division into separate training periods (see page 34). As always, it is important to adhere to fundamental principles and to use the proper type of exercises for a given method.

Principles of Training

- Basic aerobic endurance is best achieved with a period of prolonged duration with pulse rates from 140 to 170 beats per minute; in professional soccer, this is also the case with the intensive interval method (see page 32).
- Anaerobic short- and medium-duration periods are combined with the intensive interval method; this method is adapted by using soccer-specific game plays.
- Intensive (aerobic) and special stress-load training require good, basic endurance, which should be addressed first during pre- and mid-season training sessions.
- Endurance training for beginners and children should be low in intensity and should be conducted according to the long-term training method.
- Aerobic long-term endurance training with pulse rates of approximately 140 beats per minute and anaerobic limits with lactic-acid levels of approximately 2 mMol/1 are regenerative. These can be very important in the case of overtraining.
- Nourishment rich in carbohydrates and a life-style appropriate for athletes (sufficient amounts of sleep, sauna, massage, etc.) will positively influence the effects of training.

Aerobic Endurance Training

- Jogging with steady tempo and low intensity, pulse rates of 140 to 150 beats per minute (aerobic limit), duration of 30 to 45 minutes.
- As above with increased intensity, pulse rates 150 to 170 beats per minute (aerobic limit), dura-

Running Program According to Liesen

Professor Liesen, the medical adviser for Germany's national soccer team recommends the following tempo-changing programs for improving aerobic endurance and speed:

1. Start with approximately five to eight minutes relaxed trotting with stretching and loosening-up exercises.
2. Change to jogging for approximately 10 minutes.
3. Gymnastics, loosening-up, and stretching exercises (particularly for the legs), six to eight stretches per muscle group is sufficient.
4. Relaxed trotting with three to five increases of 60 to 120 feet (20–40 m) each; at least 100 yards (300 m) slow jogging between every increase.
5. Approximately five sprints over 30 to 60 feet (10–20 m) or ten sprints over 15 to 30 yards (5–10 m) with maximum intensity (from different starting positions); slow jogging for 70 yards (200 m) after every sprint.
6. Above is followed by three to five minutes of relaxed jogging.
7. Running five sets of hurdles consisting of 10 hurdles each with maximum intensity; slow jogging for 135 yards (300 m) between each hurdle.
8. Approximately 10 minutes' aerobic jogging with special emphasis on deep, rhythmic breathing; players must still be able to talk to each other.
9. Slow jogging for at least five minutes.

Physical Fitness and Fitness Training

Age-dependent Training of Fitness Skills (Male Youth)

Fitness skills	6–10 years	10–12 years	12–14 years	14–16 years	16–18 years	> 18 years
Maximum power				O	OO	OOO
Speed			O	OO	OOO →	
Endurance				O	OO	OOO
Aerobic endurance		O	OO	OO	OOO →	
Anaerobic endurance				O	OO	OOO
Anticipated speed			O	OO	OO	OOO
Reaction speed	O	OO	O	OO	OOO →	
Speed without ball	O	OO	OO	OOO →		
Speed with ball		O	OO	OO	OOO →	
Agility	OOO	OOO	OO	OO	OO →	
Coordination	O	OO	OO	OOO	OOO →	

O	Start of training with low stress load and playful training methods.
OO	Performance training with increased stress load and varied, general, and specific training methods.
OOO	Performance training with high stress load and general and special training methods during the pre-season and during the competition season.

tion of 20 to 30 minutes.

- As above with alternating tempo, varying pulse rates.
- Timed running around a square of 4 by 150 feet (4 × 50 m); time instructions given at every corner.
- All game plays, five-on-five up to eight-on-eight.
- Technical training without breaks (i.e., constantly passing balls over 150 to 200 feet (30–40 m) while running.

Anaerobic Endurance Training
Here, the types of methods recommended for power-energy and speed are also useful, if used according to the extensive and intensive interval method. Anaerobic endurance is achieved by using game plays with only a few participants (i.e., one-on-one, two-on-two, one-on-two); also highly intensive, complex exercises and relay races with and without a ball.

High-performance soccer. Results of game analysis (supported by videotapes) by Waldemar Winkler (UEFA Cup Games HSV Hamburg against Inter Milano, 1984). The results are approximately 30 to 40 percent higher than comparable studies conducted by Winkler in 1981, and 280 percent higher than those by PALFAI in 1962. Since 1962, the average increase in performance is approximately 10 percent per year.

Players (Club)	Halves	Running Distance in Yards/Metres				
		Walking	Jogging	Running fast	Running very fast	Totals
Altobelli (Inter Milano)	1st	1170 (1896 m)	1706 (1560 m)	1115 (1024 m)	601 (550 m)	5501 (5030 m)
	2nd	1972 (2070 m)	1569 (1435 m)	883 (807 m)	793 (725 m)	5508 (5037 m)
Rummenigge (Inter Milano)	1st	2187 (2288 m)	1149 (1051 m)	470 (430 m)	420 (384 m)	4541 (4153 m)
	2nd	2380 (2177 m)	1155 (1056 m)	503 (460 m)	284 (260 m)	4323 (3953 m)
Wuttke (HSV)	1st	2287 (2091 m)	2083 (1905 m)	932 (852 m)	544 (497 m)	5846 (5345 m)
	2nd	2099 (1920 m)	2118 (1937 m)	610 (558 m)	618 (565 m)	5445 (4980 m)
van Heesen (HSV)	1st	869 (795 m)	4969 (4544 m)	1469 (1343 m)	544 (497 m)	7850 (7179 m)
	2nd	865 (791 m)	4579 (4187 m)	1652 (1511 m)	598 (547 m)	7695 (7036 m)
Brady* *substituted for after 56 minutes of the game (Inter Milano)	1st	1657 (1515 m)	3162 (2891 m)	1303 (1192 m)	488 (446 m)	6610 (6044 m)
Magath** **substituted for after 70 minutes of the game (HSV)	1st	984 (900 m)	3892 (3559 m)	1877 (1716 m)	713 (652 m)	7466 (6827 m)

Physical Fitness and Fitness Training

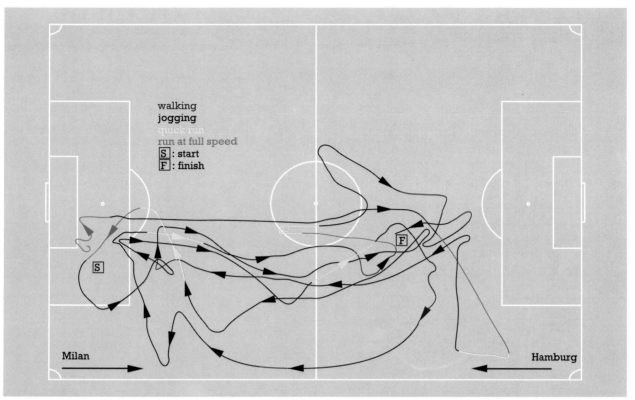

walking
jogging
quick run
run at full speed
S : start
F : finish

Milan

Hamburg

The enormous distance van Heesen covered in the span of only five minutes during the game between HSV Hamburg and Inter Milano (1984).

Aerobic endurance training with relaxed jogging.

Physical Fitness and Fitness Training

Flexibility and Flexibility Training

The importance of agility in the performance of individual techniques has already been discussed. In addition, agility affects motor skills such as power, stamina, and speed, and it is vital for well-coordinated complex movements.

> Flexibility is a player's ability to use one or more joints to perform sweeping movements, either alone or with the support of outside forces.

(The term "flexibility" also implies both agility and suppleness.)

In practical terms, we distinguish between two types of flexibility:
• Active flexibility.
• Passive flexibility.

Active Flexibility—The greatest, widest-possible movement of a joint that a player can accomplish, through his own effort, with the (abductor) muscles of that joint.

Passive Flexibility—The greatest, widest-possible movement of a joint that a player can accomplish, with the help of outside forces (a partner, a ball, etc.), by contracting the opposite (abductor) muscle of that joint. Passive agility is always greater than active; for that reason, it is important not only to do stretching exercises, but to include those that strengthen the abductor muscles.

As an Aside

Biological Prerequisites— Flexibility training can only be conducted effectively if the basic anatomical-physiological prerequisites for flexibility are in place, or at least in the developing stages. The following factors influence flexibility:

Structure of the Joint
The way joints can be moved differs according to their structure. Soccer training is not able to change this structure.

Muscle Mass
Well-developed muscles are not detrimental to good flexibility, as long as muscle-building training is combined with flexibility training.

Muscle Tone
Muscle tone (the degree to which a muscle can be tightened) has a great influence on flexibility. Muscle tone is guided by muscle spindles (running parallel to the muscle fibres) via the central nervous system. A muscle tightens or tenses up because of:
• Fatigue.
• Prolonged rest (sleep).
• Psychological excitement (for instance, prior to the start of a game).

Elasticity of a Muscle
The elasticity of a muscle depends on the degree of stretch resistance that the structure of the muscle and connective tissue allow. For example, the stretch resistance of muscle is reduced by 20 percent if the temperature increases by only three degrees Fahrenheit (two degrees Celsius).

Elasticity of Tendons and Ligaments
The movement of a joint is limited by muscles as well as by ligaments and tendons. As with muscle fibres, these tissues have different degrees of elasticity, which can be improved with proper training.

Influence of Temperature
As has already been mentioned, muscle flexibility increases when the body temperature increases. This can be accomplished by:
• Active warm-ups.
• Massages.
• An increase in the outside temperature (taking a hot bath).
• Warm clothing.

Importance for the Player

A soccer player needs good, basic flexibility in the shoulder and hip joints as well as the spinal column. However, depending on the techniques used, he has to be particularly flexible in specific joints.

Flexibility and the Instep Kick
A ball can only be kicked hard *and* low at the same time, if the player has good flexibility in his ankle joint. If the ankle joint is not flexible enough (see photos opposite page), the ball will always move in an upward curve, and shots on goal that travel 50 to 60 feet (16–20 m) will sail over the goal.

Flexibility and the Hip-Turn Kick
A hip-turn kick requires pronounced passive and active flexibility. For the high extension of the leg, the muscles (abductors) must be strengthened. The elasticity of the muscles on the inside of the thigh (abductors) can be improved by stretching exercises.

Physical Fitness and Fitness Training

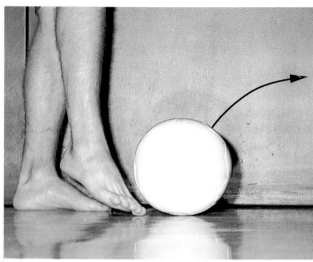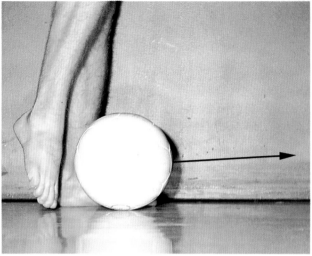

The position of the pivot leg and the way the foot is held will determine the direction of the flight of the ball.

Flexibility and Tackling

When compared to other soccer-specific techniques, hook and slide tackling are difficult movements. A player can only perform these well if his hip joints have the necessary flexibility. Relevant exercises are discussed on pages 80 and 81.

Flexibility and Dribbling

A soccer player who can't perform quick pendulum-like movements of the upper body is said to be "stiff in the hips." This statement is only partially correct. The ability to do this movement of the upper body is controlled by well-developed muscles of the body (stomach muscles and long back muscles). So-called "hip-stiff" players can overcome weak flexibility with specific power training of the relevant muscle groups.

Flexibility Training

Loss of flexibility is age-related and starts early—at about the age of 12. Training, therefore, should take place regularly, daily if possible. Since flexibility exercises are comparably easy, players should do them regularly at home. About 10 standard exercise, taking about 15 to 20 minutes, is all that is needed. We distinguish between three different methods:

Active Flexibility Exercises

Here, the player exercises with swinging, bouncing movements, moving as far as the joints will permit. Even though muscles, tendons, and ligaments are not stretched equally with the stretching method (discussed later), this method has enormous advantages because it strengthens the muscles that move joints, increasing both active elasticity and active flexibility.

In addition, these exercises teach muscles (with the help of the muscle spindle) to contract before a muscle is overstretched. This reflexive action is particularly important in soccer because of the many abrupt changes in direction.

Passive Flexibility Exercises

Here, specific muscle groups are stretched much farther (with outside support, such as a partner) than is possible with active exercises. The disadvantages is that muscles that are being moved are not strengthened. In addition, there is the danger of injury if the partner does not have enough feeling for the stretching movement the player is performing.

Static Flexibility Exercises—Stretching

This method has now found general acceptance in soccer training. This is to be applauded, because proper stretching exercises are the best way to increase the flexibility of the muscular system. We will discuss here only two of the six best-known stretching exercises.

Stretching

These are the original form of stretching exercises. They are performed with slow, deliberate movements that momentarily extend the joints, which remain in that position for about two to three seconds. The player should "listen" to the muscles, "feel" the way the tension in the muscles lessens, and consciously relax.

Physical Fitness and Fitness Training

Stretching and strengthening the back muscles.

Stretching the calf muscles.

Stretching Position

Just as important is the position in which the stretching is done. The muscle that is to be stretched should not contract at the same time. For instance, attempting to stretch the back muscle of the thigh by bending forward is useless, because this large muscle group is also carrying the weight of the upper body. The exercise causes pain, but the contracted muscle cannot be stretched.

Tightening—Relaxing—Stretching

In this method, the muscle to be stretched is first isometrically tightened for a maximum time of 10 to 30 seconds, followed by 2 to 3 seconds of total relaxing, and then stretched for another 20 to 30 seconds. The muscles will relax better after they've had a chance to contract. The stretching action that follows is then much more effective.

Stretching the muscles in the area of the hip.

Stretching the knee-bending muscles.

Physical Fitness and Fitness Training

Stretching leg, torso, and back muscles.

Stretching knee muscles.

Active stretching of the knee-bending muscle.

Active stretching of the abductor.

Stretching the abductor.

Flexibility Training Program to Do at Home

1. Stretching the musculature of the hip in the supine position (see photo opposite page).
2. Stretching the muscles of the hip joint and knee (quadriceps), from a standing or kneeling position.
3. Stretching the knee-bending muscles and the calf muscles (see photo opposite page).
4. Stretching the gluteal and back muscles by stretching in a sitting position.
5. Stretching the abductor muscle while standing (see photo opposite page).
6. Stretching the gluteal, hip-bending, and knee-stretching muscles in cross-legged position.
7. Stretching the intercostal muscles and the upper spine.
8. Stretching the hip-joint stretching muscle while simultaneously strengthening the hip-joint bending muscle with vigorous jumping; stretching the legs up and out, alternating between the left and right leg.
9. Stretching the abductor muscles while simultaneously strengthening the abductor muscle by jumping and stretching the legs up and sideways, alternating between the left and right leg (see middle photo at right).
10. Jumping jacks with alternate leg splits, scissors crossing, and knee bends.

Physical Fitness and Fitness Training

Coordination and Coordination Training

Throughout this book and particularly during the discussion of techniques and technical training, we have stressed the importance of well-developed, general coordination skills.

Coordination is the ability of a player to handle soccer-specific as well as general situations confidently, economically, and speedily. Thus, we distinguish between specific and general coordination.

Well-coordinated movements require good interactions between the nervous and muscular systems. This leads to fluid, harmonious movements that use energy economically.

Factors Influencing Coordination and Their Meaning for the Player

General coordination allows a player to handle and solve unusual situations that develop suddenly. For instance, after being fouled by an opponent, the player will roll rather than fall, and thereby avoid an injury. With well-developed specific coordination skills, he can continue dribbling successfully, even when pressured by two or more opponents, by using quick leg work, clever fakes, sudden turns, and changes of direction.

Well-coordinated movements are influenced by very different factors. The most important for a player are:

Orientation Skills (sense of direction)

This skill is particularly important for the goalkeeper. For example, when he needs to catch the ball and is pressured from the side, or when he needs to return to the goal area and the narrow penalty area is crowded with his own teammates and opponents.

Sense of Timing

To be able to head or kick an incoming pass, a player must be able to judge the distance, speed, and flight path of the ball. Players with little experience have problems judging the flight path of a ball that has been kicked with spin. They often are unable to coordinate their own reactions and movements. Good timing can only be achieved if a player has been given enough opportunities to practise judging a ball's movements. Good timing is necessary for other situations as well. For instance, when a pass is not kicked directly to a teammate but into an "empty" space, a player has to time the sprinting speed of the receiver, the speed of the ball, and the space available before the ball reaches the goal line.

Combination Skills

The mark of an elegant soccer player is the ability to combine different techniques with fluid motion. These skills are constantly demanded when faking, starting, falling and starting again, darting sideways, etc. During each of these movements, the ball has to be handled differently. From the example given above, the importance of combination skills becomes clear.

Power, Speed, Reaction, and Endurance

We have already said that basic motor skills are a fundamental requirement for well-coordinated movements. Only a complex interaction between motor skills and the coordination skills required for a given situation allows the sequence of movements to be carried out effectively.

Coordination Training

To a certain degree, coordination skills develop automatically in the course of playing the game. At the same time, however, specific training in general coordination skills should be conducted for all age groups.

General Coordination Skills

A player with a good repertoire of general movement skills will usually have good coordination skills. The ability to learn new techniques depends to a great degree on general coordination skills. Children, for instance, should have the opportunity to gain experience in many different sequences of movements during the course of specific soccer training. Here, the following training methods are useful:

- All running and rough-and-tumble games.
- Basketball, handball, volleyball, and hockey games, in addition to soccer practice games.
- Exercises taken from gymnastics (for example, rolling in different directions) can be incorporated as part of the indoors training during the winter months.
- Exercises on the trampoline (also during winter training indoors).

Physical Fitness and Fitness Training

Specific Coordination Skills

Several different methods and means are used for teaching specific coordination skills.

Methodical Methods

- Ball-handling practice with random speed changes.
- Taking shots on goal with passes from the front, sides, and back, kicking with the leg that is stepping forward and keeping the other leg in the back.
- Practising fakes to the "chocolate side" and in the other direction.
- Enlarging and reducing the game space during game plays.
- Changing the dimensions of the game space, for instance, from 60 by 125 feet to 100 by 60 feet (20 × 45 to 30 × 20 m).
- Playing on snow and ice.

Combining Techniques

- Driving the ball in uninterrupted movements in different directions.
- Punching the ball into the air, rolling forward, and catching the ball at the completion of the roll, either in the air or at the moment when it hits the ground; keeping control of the ball while running.
- Running fast while carrying two balls at the same time; a slalom run through poles.

Practising Under Time Pressure and Pressure from the Opposition

- Practising all one-on-one exercises.
- Driving the ball during relay competitions.
- Dribbling while being pressured by one or more players.

When leaping to head a high ball, the player's coordination skills are called on and developed through the complex choices of movement that must be made.

Variations

- Carrying the ball without looking at it.
- During shots-on-goal practice, the coach calls the kicking technique immediately before ball contact is made.
- During shot-on-goal practice, immediately before the ball is kicked, the goalkeeper randomly vacates a corner; or the coach, standing behind the goal, gives a hand signal, informing the player into which corner the ball is to be kicked.

Practising with Additional Game Pressure

- Ball-juggling during "active" breaks of interval training—concentration and precision are important here.
- One-on-two play, dribbling towards the goal, kicking a goal—again, emphasizing concentration and precision.
- Catching a hard-kicked pass and driving the ball with a fluid motion at maximum speed.

Tactics and Tactical Training

In addition to techniques and physical fitness, tactics play an important role in achieving success in competition. Tactical planning and actions are fundamentally oriented towards the end result, which means that tactics are implemented to score goals, to prevent goals, to win the game, and to achieve the highest possible standing in the division at the end of the season.

In general, tactics are defined as:

The systematic, success-oriented implementation of actions by individual players, group of players, and teams—taking into account the level of performance skills of the team, that of the opposition, and any given situation on the field.

The term "tactics" in soccer, as well as in other sports, means different things:

- Tactics of planning, preparing, and organizing a competitive game.
- Tactics as the availability of experience and knowledge of game situations, and the use of technical, physical, and psychological methods for solving those situations.
- Tactics as a plan for specific actions.
- Tactics as a practical deployment of an action.

Depending on a given situation, tactical maneuvers can be carried out by an individual player, a group of players, or by the entire team.

The table on page 86 gives an overview of the many tactical maneuvers available to the team. We distinguish between:

- Team tactics (see page 91).
- Group tactics (see page 97).
- Individual tactics (see page 105).
- Game tactics (see page 119).
- Tactics for standard situations (see page 124).
- Tactics for a given day (see page 134).

Tactical maneuvers in a game situation depend on two things: Does the player have possession of the ball or must he first regain possession? Accordingly, we distinguish between:

- Offensive tactics.
- Defensive tactics.

Since all tactical maneuvers take place within a specific game plan, these are discussed later (see page 137).

Tactical Tasks of Players and Management

According to the expanded meaning of the term "tactics," the responsibility for the success of the team depends not only on its players and coach, but also on the management. What follows is a discussion of the responsibilities for the different tasks of the owner, board, manager, physician, masseur, coach, and players in the planning and preparing for competition.

Owner, Board, Manager, Physician, Masseur, and Coach

- Travel plans for out-of-town games.
- Setting up training camps and making hotel reservations.
- Arrangements for food and drink for the day before the match and the day of the match.
- Provisions for extreme weather conditions (cold: tights, gloves, headbands; heat: special liquids, ice bags, etc.).
- Choice of outfits (adjusted to given situations; i.e., light-colored game uniforms for night games).
- Proper preparation for games played in another country (for instance, proper immunization, arrivals scheduled to guarantee sufficient time for acclimatization, sufficient amounts of germ-free water, etc.).

Additional Responsibilities of the Coach

- Analysis of the opposing team (lineup, game strategy, playing methods, strengths and weaknesses of individual players).
- Designing game tactics with respect to the opposition and environmental situation.
- Establishing the lineup according to game tactics.
- Evaluating the state of each player and acting accordingly (calming down or pepping up).
- Choosing the proper equipment (shoes, type of cleats).
- Overseeing warm-ups.
- Providing drinks for the break (tea, electrolyte-replacement drinks).

Additional Responsibilities of Players

- Analyzing the probable strengths and weaknesses of the opponent.
- Mental preparation for the match and the opponent.
- Testing the condition of the playing field and deciding on proper shoes.
- Attitude adjustments before the game.

Tactics and Tactical Training

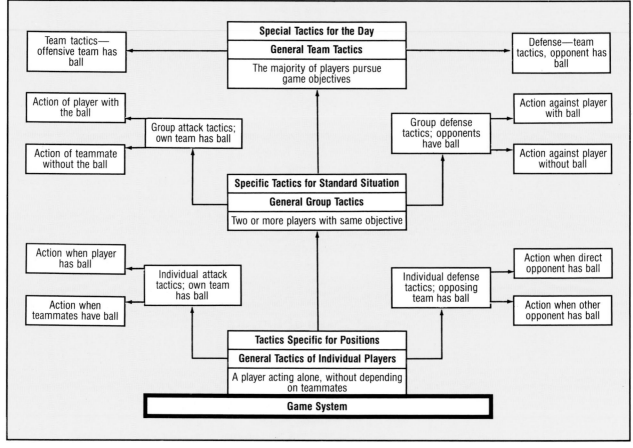

Team tactics— offensive team has ball	**Special Tactics for the Day**	Defense—team tactics, opponent has ball
	General Team Tactics	
	The majority of players pursue game objectives	

Schematic overview of the different types of tactical maneuver.

Influences on Tactics

Planning and preparing for a match, the choice of game tactics, and the actual play of the game are influenced by several different factors.

Those influencing tactical maneuvers of the whole team are:
- Long-term strategy of the team and the present standing in the division.
- The actual objective of the game being played (i.e., win, win by a large margin, draw, or even losing by only one point).
- The actual state of the team (for instance, the psychological and physical state, the lineup, etc.).
- The opponents and their state

(i.e., place in the division, lineup, strategy, tactics, strengths and weaknesses, and personalities of the players).
- The type of match (i.e., training game, exhibition match, championship game, etc.).
- Day and time of the game (i.e., Wednesday–Friday schedule, daylight, night game under lights, etc.).
- Place where the game is played (i.e., at home, away, in another country, under unusual weather conditions, on a field that is used for training only, etc.).
- The expectations of the spectators.
- The way a particular referee handles the rules of the game.

In addition to the factors that influence all players, each individual player will choose his own, unique tactics, taking the following into consideration:
- His personal goal, such as making up for a prior poor performance, securing his place on the team, impressing the coach from the opposing team with a spectacular performance (trade!), impressing the fans, the press, etc.
- His own physical shape that day.
- The strengths and weaknesses of his direct opponent.

Further discussion of these factors can be found in the section on "Tactics for the Day," page 134.

Tactics and Tactical Training

Tactical Maneuvering— Tactical Skills

For the spectator, a tactical maneuver appears to take only seconds, often only fractions of a second. The fan notices only the small, visible part of the action. This visible phase is preceded by a number of other phases. A player must go through those phases perfectly, if the outcome of the visible phase is to be successful. In order to do this, other skills, besides techniques and physical fitness, are necessary.

Sequence of a Tactical Maneuver

Tactical action can be performed by individual players, groups of players, or the whole team. The complexity of the action demands mental, psychological, and physical commitment from a player. The table below explains the different phases:

Phase 1—Assumes any number of game situations. Here, for instance, a midfielder just received the ball.

Phase 2—A player needs sensory capabilities, such as good peripheral vision, tactile senses, muscle sense, equilibrium, and a sense of space and position. In order to use these skills, a player must be motivated and have concentration.

Phases 3 and 4—A player needs intelligence in the form of knowledge, memorization of events taking place on the field, creativity, foresight, and the ability to make mental adjustments.

Phase 5—Willingness becomes concrete action, and the established game plan takes shape. For

this, the player needs self-assurance, calmness, consistency, assertiveness, the ability to function under stress and to remain undisturbed when interfered with, courage, the willingness to take risks and to make decisions, and determination.

Phase 6—It is here that the mental and psychological factors produce visual motor actions. Technical skills, fitness, and coordination skills will determine the quality of the actions. But emotional qualities, such as self-control, stamina, and courage, influence the success of the action.

Phases 7a and 7b—Here again, mental skills are necessary in order to critically analyze and memorize the cause and effect of those actions. Unless a player has the ability to unemotionally and self-critically distance himself from the actions, this phase will not be very successful.

Schematic Model of the Sequence of Tactical Actions, with Practical Examples of the Phases

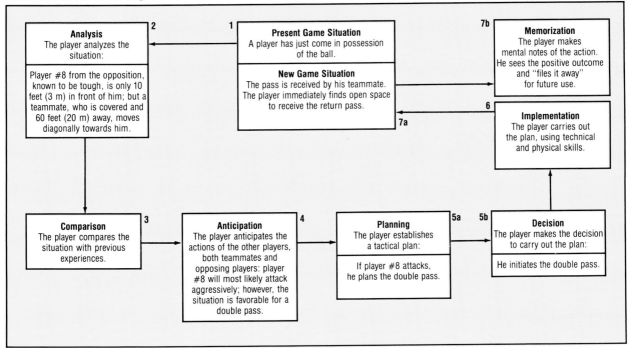

Tactics and Tactical Training

Tactical Ability

In summary, here are the factors that affect tactical ability:

Motivational Factors
Need, motivation, emotion, interest, attitude.

Sensory Factors
Peripheral vision, focused vision, spatial-related auditory sense, tactile sense, equilibrium.

Intellectual Abilities
Knowledge (rules, typical game situations, and solutions that have proven successful), ability to concentrate, keeping track of game events, thinking ahead, planning ahead, creativity.

Character and Temperament
Forcefulness, willingness to endure, self-assurance, courage, willingness to take risks, conscientiousness, ability to achieve, optimism, ability to act.

Tactical Training

The tactical ability of a player, and by extension, of the team, depends on many different, but very basic factors. These factors cannot be improved by using only one method. Basically, we have to distinguish between the following:
- The training of motivational and emotional abilities.
- The training of intellectual abilities.
- The development of practical aspects and fitness, as well as all other factors involved in taking practical actions.

The following examples are meant as suggestions for a deliberate training of tactical skills by coaches and players alike. However, it is not possible to discuss every method.

In talking with the players the coach can help develop their tactical abilities.

Improving Motivation

Needs, motives, emotions, interests, and attitudes are different for each player and can only be assessed during one-on-one discussions. General appeals, such as those made during halftime or at players' meetings, are only supplements. Players must be educated about the connection between motivation and tactical abilities. True motivation is usually achieved with a few, pointed remarks. Often, however, motivation is ruined by too many instructions or by instructions that are too complicated.

Also, fatigue has a negative influence on the ability to concentrate. Therefore, a proper balance between practice and rest during training and a proper lifestyle are prerequisites if the following are to be effective.

The level of a team's motivation is proof of the quality of a coach.

Tactics and Tactical Training

Improving Sensory Abilities

Anyone who has had a chance to watch a game played by deaf players will appreciate the importance of *all* senses performing effectively.

Although the degree to which a player is able to use his senses is influenced by heredity, in the context of this discussion we believe that improvements are possible. Other prerequisites for an effective training program are lifestyle (sufficient sleep, no alcohol or nicotine, etc.) and an adherence to the principle of optimum balance between stress load and recuperation.

Peripheral vision is reduced when training sessions are held on a field or based solely on abbreviated game plays. To be able to effectively sense the position of the opponent and to anticipate his attack, tactile senses should be trained by organizing game plays in a smaller space, preferably where one side outnumbers the other.

The ability to quickly assess a game situation can be improved by making up "provocation" rules (i.e., contact with the ball is only allowed twice).

Kinesthetic senses, for instance, are improved when the coach demands self-correction from a player. This forces a player to pay more attention and to become more aware of the movement of his muscles.

Improving Intellectual Abilities

Improving *concentration attention* must be an ongoing part of a training program. For example, ball-juggling practice should follow an exhausting exercise or training session. The game plays we have already mentioned, where only limited ball contact is allowed, also help to improve these skills.

By introducing new kinds of game plays and exercises, a player is constantly asked to think, to adjust, and to relearn. Improved concentration is the reward, and it will have a positive effect on the player's performance during competition.

Mental training (visualization) and autogenic training will further improve concentration skills.

On one hand, *training for tactical knowledge* is the task of the coach; on the other hand, every player is responsible for generating his own means of improving this skill. Many possibilities are available. Individual as well as group discussions, using a blackboard, can be helpful. The coach can also analyze videos and films during group discussions. Players themselves can conduct a kind of "observation" training where particular situations are analyzed (i.e., actions taken by midfielders, behavior during one-on-one confrontations, use of space, switching positions and responsibilities, switching from offense to defense, standard game situations, etc.). As previously mentioned, mental training can take place at home in the form of visualization. The player, in his mind, goes through one-on-one, double passing, and standard strategies. Memorization will not improve simply by playing and repeating plays. To become an above-average player, he must go over the game and its specific situations in his mind after the game, "see" the way particular actions developed, and how they proceeded. Cause and effect, reactions, and his own performance need to be critically analyzed. Praise and reprimands from the coach strengthen the experience if they are given objectively.

Improving Character Traits and Temperamental Behavior

For many tactical strategies, character traits such as courage, willingness to take risks, calmness, self-confidence, and responsibility are immensely important.

A coach should be a strong example. An anxious coach will have anxious players; a coach who is not afraid to take risks has players who love to take risks.

It is important to help a player trust his own performance and his ability to perform. This can only be accomplished during one-on-one discussions. The coach might want to encourage the player to take the risks necessary for the successful completion of a task (dribbling, long passes, etc.). At the same time, the coach needs to give the player and his teammates assurance that even if a risky play did not work out, his willingness to try is still viewed in a positive light.

The necessary *sense of responsibility* can be instilled by giving players a say in and responsibility for matters affecting the game. The coach must assign specific responsibilities to each player.

Tactics and Tactical Training

Emotion, the need to compensate, egotism, and fatigue all block responsible behavior. A coach should address these negative tendencies early on.

Calmness and composure are traits that are particularly important during decisive games. Positive comments called in by the coach during such games are very effective. Critical comments during the game and during halftime are usually counterproductive; however, if necessary, they should be objective and given in the form of suggestions. Fear of a possible loss, or even a loss in the standings, should be discussed *before* the game. When the question of losing is brought up, it usually turns out that the consequences would not be all that dramatic (at least in youth and amateur leagues).

Calmness and composure don't have to be abandoned in the course of a game that the team is losing. Armed with inner confidence, a player will be able to overcome pregame stress. One-on-one talks with a player are very helpful here. Assigning concrete and specific tasks will help remove fear. A player will know that he is not alone with the responsibility assigned to him, when his coach reminds him of the importance of teamwork. Furthermore, sufficient warm-up, stretching exercises, and massages will help achieve overall relaxation.

From the above discussion, it is clear that individual attention from the coach can have a positive effect on a player's performance in many ways. One-on-one talks are among the most important measures a coach has at his disposal.

Practice of Complex Tactical Skills

The actual training of complex tactical skills has many technical components. The following methods are useful:
- Standard combinations.
- Double passing, wall play.
- Complex exercises.
- Game play, one-plus-two-on-two.
- Game practice on small and regulation-size fields.
- Exhibition games.
- Point games.

Which of these methods is best? That will depend primarily on the performance level of the players. Complex exercises and small game plays are best for strong players. Since these players already have a large tactical repertoire, it is sufficient to correct mistakes during breaks.

However, beginners and young players can only acquire proper tactical skills (i.e., combinations) with methodical, step-by-step instructions. The following steps are necessary:

1. Learning and practising the technical elements that are necessary for tactical maneuvers.
2. Introduction of combinations through demonstrations, instructions, and explanations.
3. Practising combinations, first without an opponent, later with an opponent (active and semi-active).
4. Introducing and practising a variation of combination plays or a second variation of the same combination.
5. Alternating practice of two or more basic forms or variations with an active opponent (opponent does not know which variation has been chosen).
6. Trying out different forms of combination plays as part of conducting complex exercises during small game plays.
7. Using a combination play during training games.
8. Application of tactics in competitive games.

The coach must constantly remind players to make conscious use of the newly acquired tactical skills during competitive games, since they will be inclined to use only those skills that they have already mastered.

Tactics and Tactical Training

Team Tactics

Team tactics are defined as the purposeful, planned offensive and defensive actions of all the players on a team.

Actions that are carried out by an individual and a group together are part of a more complex structure. Team tactics include the following actions:

Offensive Tactics—own team is in possession of the ball
- Alternating tempo and rhythm of the action.
- Manipulating the space.
- Alternating technical methods.
- Playing for time.
- Counterattack.
- Frontal attack.

Defensive Tactics—opponents are in possession of the ball
- Playing for time (see page 94).
- Covering opponent, space, and mixed coverage (see page 92).
- Fore-checking in the opponent's half of the field (see page 95).
- Drawing back to your own half of the field (see page 95).

Alternating Tempo and Rhythm of the Game

Successful teams will use both technical and tactical methods in a constantly changing pattern during the course of a game. This makes it difficult for the opponents to stick to their strategy.

Well-planned changes of tempo and rhythm are the mark of a top team. Teams that are constantly attacking with fast passes often don't have enough strength left at the end of a game to withstand the pressure of an aggressive op-

ponent. The opposition will have no problem adjusting its own strategy accordingly; they will wait patiently for the right time to attack. On the other hand, an opponent might be caught by surprise when, after having passed the ball back and forth for some length of time, a dribbling player suddenly breaks through. By the way, this strategy is characteristic of the Brazilian national team.

Manipulation of Space

Inexperienced teams usually start their offense in the part of the field where they took possession of the ball. It is inevitable that they will run into a tightly organized opposition, because their attack begins in the midst of the greatest number of opponents. Changing sides should only take place in midfield when it is safe to do so, because a square pass in front of one's own goal is *the* deadly sin of soccer—it always brings the opposition dangerously close to the goal.

Alternating Technical Methods

Alternating the tempo and rhythm of the game is usually connected to a change in techniques. The team that always uses the same technique becomes predictable and is easy to defeat. Therefore, the game strategy of a team should always alternate between:
- Short and long passes.
- Combination plays and dribbling.
- Shooting from the second line, double-pass combinations into the penalty area of the opposition, etc.

By practising across large spaces with all these elements, players learn the deliberate changes from one technique to another.

Playing for Time

When a team is leading, or if it is outnumbered due to an injury or a penalty, and the game is almost over, the team will play for time or stall to prevent the opposition from scoring. In addition, the counterattack (see next subject) and strong combination plays in midfield or in the opponent's half of the field are particularly successful. It is important that the play not be taken to the opponent's goal. The team simply passes the ball back and forth in a way that appears to be totally unplanned and random. However, it is important that the players do not fall asleep. As many players as is practical should participate in the combination plays, which means they must be constantly moving about and ready to receive the ball at any time. If players lose concentration and become inattentive during the playing-for-time maneuver, they leave themselves wide open to a counterattack by the opposition.

Counterattack and Frontal Attack

When a team has gained possession of the ball, the attack on the opponent's goal can take two different forms:

Counterattack—Here, the strategy is to reach the opponent's half of the field with long diagonal or through passes, or by fast drib-

Tactics and Tactical Training

A Comparison of Counterattacks and Frontal Attacks

	Counterattack	Frontal Attack
Objectives	Basic defense	Reliable combination plays
	Strong defense	Quick defenders (own), reliably covering sweeper
	Quick change from defense to offense	
Tasks	Good sprinter	Good technician
Requirements	Calm goalkeeper	Close cooperation between players
Advantages	Lots of room for own quick-footed forward	Ball control through reliable passes
	Opponent is tricked into making mistakes due to own defensive action	Because of this: more fun
		Play-for-time possible, advantage in connection with forechecking
	Own offense possible due to good defense, chance to surprise opponent	
Disadvantages	Forwards are on their own	Space for forwards is limited
	Little cooperation between team players	Danger: counterattack by the opponents
	Risky through passes, easy to catch by opponent	Reduces chance to reach opponents' goal

Coverage of the Opponent and Space

The tactic of covering a player, a space, and a combination of the two has significance for group tactics. The principles of these tactics are also valid when every player of the team is involved in covering his respective opponent.

Covering a player means that after the team has lost possession of the ball, *each* player must proceed immediately towards his respective opponent. The closer the opponent is to reaching the goal with the ball, the tighter the coverage must be. If only one player switches to defense, the whole defensive strategy is in jeopardy, since something like a chain reaction is set in motion, where a player thinks he is not just responsible for covering his own opponent, but also for covering his "neighbor's" opponent.

bling through the midfield. Especially effective is a counterattack that not only sets the action in motion but gets the ball into the opponent's half of the field at the same time.

Frontal Attack—Here, the tempo is much slower. Midfield is not the place for long, risky passes; rather, players should use the safe relay method, covering short distances with each pass. For the frontal attack, many more offensive players have to be involved than for a counterattack. Defenders, midfielders, and forwards are in much closer contact during a frontal attack than a counterattack. Advantages and disadvantages are shown in the table.

In professional soccer, forwards are covered tightly and aggressively.

Tactics and Tactical Training

When *covering space* after losing the ball, every player involved in the offensive actions should immediately proceed back to his own zone. Midfield players and forwards who have moved diagonally out of their zone during offensive actions can (after checking with their "neighbors," who are changing defensive positions) move straight back, and temporarily cover the zone of a different opponent.

For *combination coverage*, in addition to covering the center forward positions, players often also have to cover a specific, individual opponent, as dictated by the situation at hand. Players taking over this coverage only play a limited role in their team's offensive actions. In this way, if their team should lose possession of the ball, they can immediately switch back to one-on-one coverage of their respective opponent.

Playing for Time by Destroying the Opposition's Game Plan

Another form of playing for time at the end of a game is to destroy the game plan of the opposition. This method is used when a team wants to preserve a narrow lead, save the day with a tie, or has little energy left to mount a counterattack. Here, a team will try to disrupt the flow of the opponents' game. Often, the methods used to accomplish the task are not very attractive. The so-called "kick and rush" method moves the ball across the field in the direction of the opponents' goal without any real plan; however, it is best to use diagonal passes in the direction of the corner flag on the opposite side of the field. Teammates following the action have the best chance of catching up with the ball.

Another way of destroying the opponents' game is to use an offside kick, or even to kick the ball beyond the goal line. In both cases, it is hoped that during the seconds it takes to get the ball back into play the defense has regrouped. Generally, this type of play is not recommended. In modern soccer, where we talk about planned tactical strategies, there is little justification for it. A designed plan (see page 91) could achieve the same effect. However, soccer also claims that the end justifies the means (if the players remain within the rules). In special situations, it is acceptable to use the "destructive" game plan.

Comparison of One-on-One and Space Coverage

	One-on-one coverage	Covering space
Objectives	Every player covers his respective opponent	Every player covers the opponent in *his* zone
Tasks	Good endurance	Every player moves towards the ball
		Attack of ballcarrier by two or more players at the same time
Requirements	Disciplined coverage by all defenders and midfielders	Accepting or turning over coverage if opponent goes to another zone
Advantages	Clearly defined tasks; no question of responsibility	Economical movement, saves energy
	Concentrating on *one* opponent	Same starting position for all players for own offensive action
	Vulnerable opponent	Method gives better mutual support than one-on-one coverage
	Opponent has his back to his own goal	Consequently: better chance for wall and double pass
Disadvantages	Opponent determines the "march route"	Space is only a mental concept
	Therefore: interruption of defensive plan because of position changes	Susceptible to dribbling at the border line of zones
	Vulnerable to quick opposing forwards	Susceptible when game action switches to the opposite side
		Changing opponents
		Opponents not challenged when regaining ball

Tactics and Tactical Training

Fore-checking

This team tactic, used in ice hockey, has also found its way into the game of soccer. When a team has lost the ball and is still in the opponents' half of the field, every player becomes involved in the attempt to regain possession of the ball. Usually, the ballcarrier is pressed (see page 105) by two or more players, while the rest provide coverage of the space in the vicinity of the ball. This tactic only works if the defenders also move to midfield, creating close contact with players in every position.

Falling Back

The extreme opposite of fore-checking is "falling back." With this tactic, the ballcarrier from the opposing team is attacked with a stalling technique to give as many teammates as possible time to get back and guard their own goal. Then, a solid defense, several lines deep, is organized. Because of this tight defense, the ballcarrier is forced to the touch line or has to use square passes in front of the defensive line.

Fore-checking and falling back are defensive strategies that have their advantages and disadvantages. They have been compared in the table on this page.

Which method to choose always depends on the team's ability.

Comparison of Fore-checking (pressing) and Falling Back

	Defense with fore-checking (pressing)	Defense by falling back (to own goal line)
Objective	Rapidly regaining the ball while still in opponents' zone	Securing own goal while opponent still has ball
Task	Attacking ballcarrier with several players (pressing)	Counterattacking from own defensive line
	Aggressive use of all players	
Prerequisite	Close contact among all players	Pretending attack on ballcarrier
	Quick defense to avoid opponents' counterattack	Basic defensive formation
Advantages	Quickly regaining possession of the ball; opposition cannot "steal" time	Counterattack from opposition is easier to handle
	Short running distances when switching to defense	Tightened space of opposing forwards
	Effective against weak opponent	Very effective when space coverage is used
	Good for team that uses frontal attack	Good position for starting offense
Disadvantages	Susceptible to counterattack by opponent	Opposition in midfield keeps ball unhindered
	Own forward constantly under pressure	Opposition dictates game rhythm

Tactics and Tactical Training

Group Tactics

Group tactics are defined as purposeful, planned, offensive, and defensive cooperative actions for the purpose of solving game situations.

When individual game situations are compared to more complex ones, it becomes clear that additional methods and skills are required. Often in the course of a game, the following player groups will plan and cooperate:

- Goalie/sweeper/defender.
- Sweeper/midfielder/defender.
- Defender/midfielder.
- Midfielder/midfielder.
- Midfielder/forward.
- Forward/forward.

The type of action used to answer a given situation depends on the position of the respective players, the game strategy, team tactics, and the type of game the opposition is playing. With regard to group tactics, the following actions are necessary:

Offensive Tactics:
Action of the Player with the Ball

- Initiate standard combination with short passes.
- Initiate double pass with a direct or delayed pass.
- Turn ball over.
- Fake kick, then dribble.
- Initiate side and wing change with long pass.

Action of Teammates

- Be available to participate in standard combinations.
- Be available for double pass.
- Be ready to receive the ball.

- Change position on the field, wide as well as deep.
- Entice opponent to leave the space he is covering.
- Run behind the opponent.

Action of Players of a Group

- Wing play.
- Shifting action to another space.
- Playing against numerous defenders.
- Overcoming offside trap.

Defensive Tactics:
Against Ball-carrying Opponent

- Tackling and protecting the goal.
- Accepting and passing on coverage of an opponent.
- Tackling by pressing with two or more teammates.
- Delaying tackling.
- Safeguarding goalkeeper on both sides, ready for second shot on goal.

Against Opponent Without the Ball

- Interrupt opponents when they change positions.
- Prevent double pass by covering space.
- Shift position in the direction of the ball.

Against the Whole Opposing Group

- Space coverage.
- Mixed coverage.
- Set offside trap.

For reasons of clarity, the list is divided into group-tactic tasks, individual tasks (i.e., action of the player with the ball), and actions against an individual player (i.e, actions against the ball-carrying

opponent). Some of these actions have also been covered under "individual tactics" (such as passing and shaking off coverage by an opponent).

What follows is a more detailed explanation of the cooperation between individual players in the overall tactical strategy of the group.

Offensive Group Tactics

Change of Position

Changing a player's position always changes the task that is connected with that particular position. In modern soccer, the following positions are exchanged:

- Across the width of the field (i.e., between forward striker or midfield players).
- Along the length or depth of the field (i.e., between midfield players and strikers or between defenders and midfield players; see photo).

Exchanging positions has the following advantages for the team in possession of the ball:

- Changing positions creates, briefly at least, two open spaces from which passes can be kicked (providing that the defensive player goes with the player who is changing).
- Opposing defenders are lured into new positions and, therefore, confronted by tasks they are not familiar with.
- The defensive strategy is at least temporarily disrupted, and the opposition is forced to regroup.
- Defending players have to shift their concentration to the change in the action; thus, they pay less attention to the opposing player they are covering.

Tactics and Tactical Training

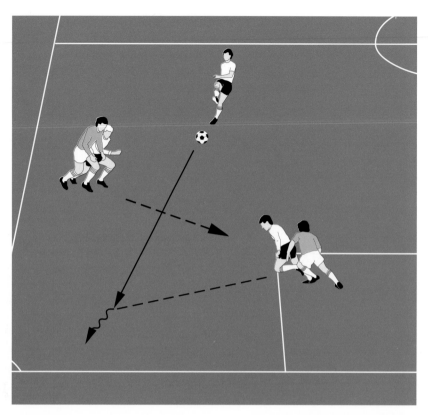

Short Pass Combination

For simple combination passes of 15 to 50 feet (5–15 m), players have a number of different tactics available. Since these combinations happen with great frequency, they are also known as *standard combinations*. They can involve two or three players. The drawings on pages 100 and 101 show the most important two- and three-player combinations.

Wall Pass and Double Pass

Both the wall pass and the double pass are more advanced forms of the standard combinations; they are meant to counter tight one-on-one coverage. They allow a forward to successfully defend himself against tight coverage and aggressive interference during a pass reception. The terms "wall pass" and "double pass" are often used interchangeably. Nevertheless, the following distinctions are often made:

- Wall pass is a combination with two passes.
- Double pass is a combination with three passes.

The photos on the opposite page show the sequence of action of a double pass (as defined above).

The basic form of the wall pass can be varied in many ways. For example, the second pass can be delayed, keeping the opposing player in the dark. Will the player go towards the goal himself or will he pass again? A particularly effective variation of the double pass is when the last pass is not kicked to the player who started the action, but to a third player (see photo opposite page).

Two players change positions: across the width of the field (above) and the length of the field (below).

Tactics and Tactical Training

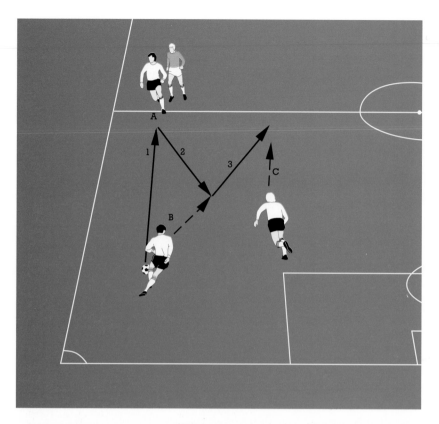

A double pass, in which the last pass goes to a third player, creating an additional moment of surprise for the opposition.

Running Behind

The so-called "running behind" tactic is a very effective variation in modern soccer. Here, the player who just kicked the pass changes space by going both deeper and wider. The second player, delaying his return pass, uses deceptive moves to kick the ball to his teammate.

"Running behind" is a tactic often used in modern soccer.

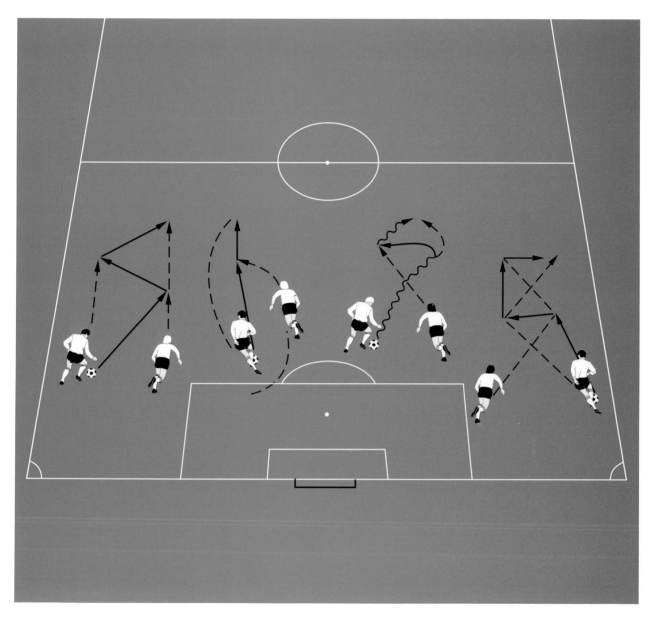

Expansive Combination

Expansive combinations are particularly useful when it is necessary to quickly cover great distances to the opponents' goal. This tactic has to be practised systematically until the moves become automatic, because this method often leads to mistakes. The drawing shows numerous, suitable combinations for groups of two and three.

Typical standard combinations (here for groups of two) are also used for training technical skills. They can be combined in various forms.

Tactics and Tactical Training

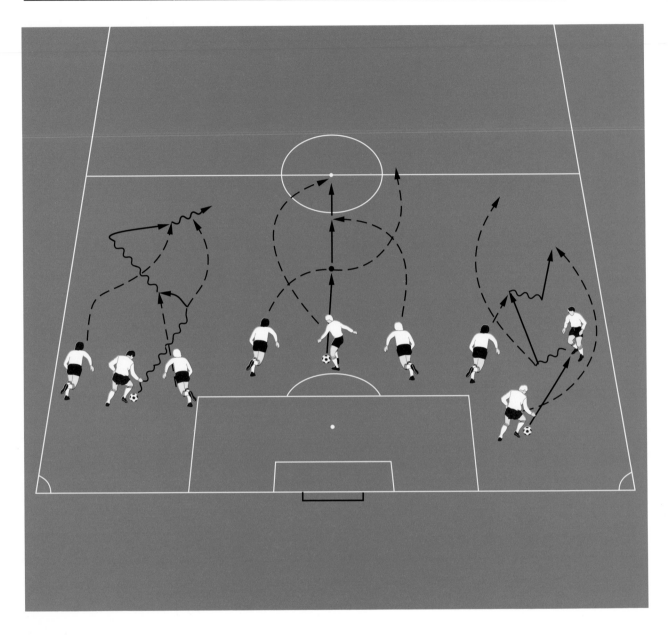

Practice of standard combinations for groups of three helps players develop a "feel" for action without the ball, for passing into open space, and for the many different ways of using open space.

Plays from Sides to Side

In modern soccer, the space in front of the goal is guarded by a mighty "wall" of several layers of defenders. Attacks from either the left or right side are, therefore, very dangerous. The objective of this kind of attack is to drive the ball through the less densely covered space and make a sharp pass to the advancing forward behind the backs of the opponents. Since the sweeper often has to leave his central position to support the defense, there is usually a teammate in the middle who is free to receive the pass.

Every basic form of open-space combination has several variations. These enrich the tactical wing strategy.

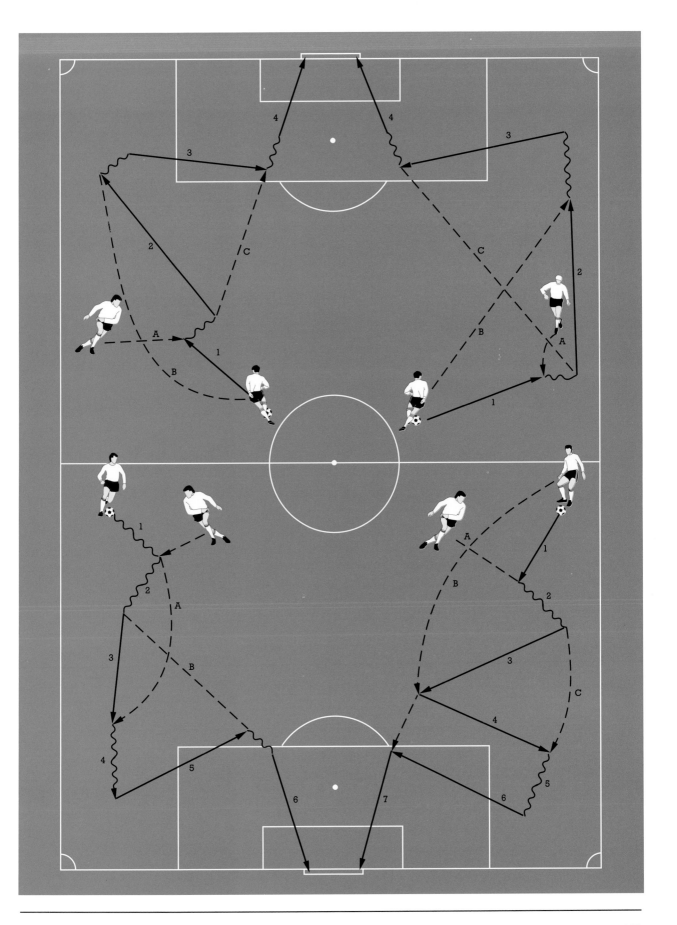

Changing the Field of Action and Switching Sides

Today, it is common for two or more players to begin to attack the ball-carrying offensive player in midfield. The rationale is to disrupt the ballcarrier and keep him from shooting a pass. The obvious result is that the defense creates a player deficit on the opposite side of the field, in spite of the fact that five or even six players operate in midfield. The pressure on the ballcarrier can be relieved by using the back pass. The receiving player in the back should follow with a diagonal flank pass, shifting the game action to the other side of the field. Often the shift from one side to the other is repeated several times within one offensive action. When the opposition gets tired from trying to catch up (and not until then), the tactic is changed, often with a through pass kicked towards the penalty area of the opposing team.

Beating the Offside Trap

The offside trap is a very effective defensive tactic for groups and for the team (see page 108). There are three basic countermeasures against the offside trap:

- High, square passes behind the forward-moving defense line. Since the ball is in the air for a relatively long time, out of reach of the opposition, midfielders have a good chance to take possession of the ball.
- Break-through dribbling from the rear. A midfielder, moved into the field of action by a back pass, attempts to break through with fast, explosive dribbling.
- Wall and double passes in a tight space. A wall pass, with delayed kick, to the center forward has the best chance for success.

Defensive Group Tactics

Safeguarding the Player Who Is on the Attack

The attack on a ball-carrying opponent, in midfield as well in the defensive line, can only be carried out aggressively and without risk if the attacker has at least one teammate for backup. This situation is typical for the combination sweeper/center forward, and the type of midfield action known as "pressing." THe following factors are important:

- The player safeguarding the teammate in the back keeps a distance of 6 to 10 feet (2–3 m).
- The two players involved make sure that the space to the left and right of the ball-carrying opponent is covered.

The attacking player should safeguard the space towards the middle, while the other player falls back somewhat to safeguard the outside.

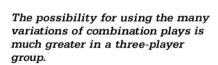

The possibility for using the many variations of combination plays is much greater in a three-player group.

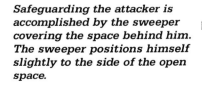

Safeguarding the attacker is accomplished by the sweeper covering the space behind him. The sweeper positions himself slightly to the side of the open space.

▷

Tactics and Tactical Training

Turning Over Coverage of an Opponent

Basically, turning over coverage to a teammate takes place when an opponent leaves the zone in which he was being covered. The switch takes place between zones. This is always a risky maneuver. Today, players usually agree not to transfer coverage when in, or directly in front of, the dangerous penalty area. Instead, they stay with the opponent they are responsible for. Coverage of the opponent must be turned over even if the player has outplayed his assigned cover. It is important that the player, who was outplayed, moves back behind his teammate (who has taken over coverage) as quickly as possible in order to support him in the one-on-one confrontation.

For teams that use team coverage, the coverage of an opponent who is about to break through is primarily the responsibility of the sweeper. He should not move too fast or get too far ahead, otherwise he loses contact with the rest of the defensive line. It is enough to prevent the opponent, who is 60 to 75 feet (20–25 m) in front of the goal from scoring. The opponent can only initiate aggressive actions if he can be supported by his teammates.

Forming an Echelon of Midfield and Defensive Players

For the group-tactic strategy discussed above, it is important that the individual players, moving in the direction of the ball, form an echelon deep enough so that they cover each other. In this way, the ballcarrier is constantly prevented from dribbling through.

Shifting Position in the Direction of the Ball

Sepp Herberger (head coach of Germany's national soccer team in 1957) demanded that more of his players be in the vicinity of the ball than players from the opposition. For teams using team coverage, this strategy is still valid today. The motto of modern soccer is: "Quickly regain possession of the ball." This is the reason why several players apply pressure on the ball-carrying opponent. This can only be accomplished when every player participates in the defensive move towards the ball. The drawing below shows the accordion-like movement of the players.

After a pass, players shift their position in the direction of the ball; the opponents closest to the ball are covered more tightly.

Tactics and Tactical Training

Coverage of Space

The fundamental difference between the coverage of a single opponent and the coverage of space is discussed under individual tactics, later in the book. While one-on-one coverage can be successfully carried out by one player, space coverage, generally, is only successful as a group or team tactic. Every player is responsible for defending a particular space (zone). He has to attack every opponent, with or without the ball, who enters this zone. If the opponent moves to another zone, the teammate assigned to that zone automatically takes over the coverage. Both methods, one-on-one and space coverage, have special advantages and disadvantages and make specific demands on the team that uses them. These requirements, disadvantages, and advantages are listed in the table on page 94.

The drawing shows one of many possible ways of dividing defensive space into zones (example of a 3–5–2 system).

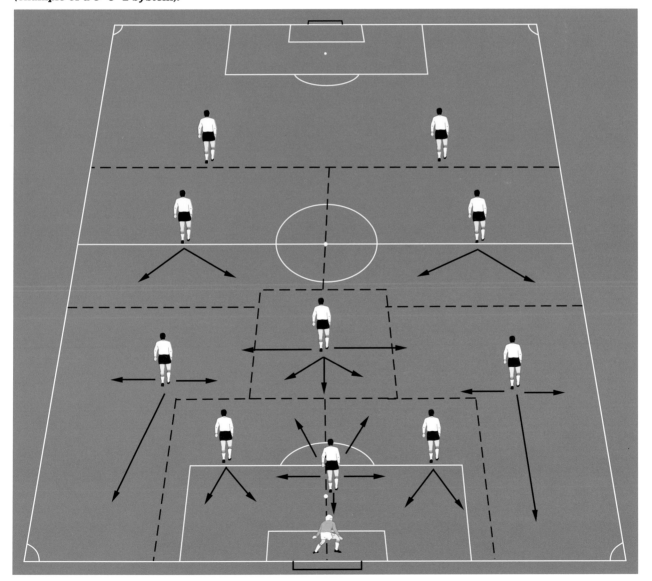

Tactics and Tactical Training

Mixed Coverage

The "space coverage" euphoria of the first half of the 80's has been replaced, primarily by mixed coverage. Here, the players in the center forward position are covered one-on-one, at least while the action is in the middle of the opposition's half of the field. In the remaining areas, players use space coverage. In theory, this sounds rather simple; however, in practice it is very difficult. Forwards are constantly on the move, and the space they leave must be covered immediately. This requires a great deal of running on the part of the midfield and defensive players, as well as great mental flexibility.

Preparing the Offside Trap

Aggressively preparing an offside trap, a tactic that involves every defensive player, has become one of the most effective defensive tactics used today. Unlike what was used in the past, the signal for the advance of the defensive players does not come from a player (i.e., from the sweeper). Rather, it is the way in which a typical game situation develops that signals an aggressive, joint move to the midline. The result is that the offside line automatically moves forward several yards. The opposing forwards are forced to react, meaning they have to retreat. This, in turn, stops any offensive move, and combinations have to be developed all over again by using back passes.

The following situations have a good chance of success when preparing an offside trap:

- When the goalie or a defender returns the ball back into the game via a corner or free kick.
- When a free kick from midfield is cleared and returned to the game.
- When an opposing player in possession of the ball is pressed and must use a back pass to protect the ball.

In every case, the defense moves aggressively forward. For this risky maneuver, it is important that a few midfielders safeguard the action by moving in scissors-like fashion towards the advancing defense in the direction of their own goal.

A Dutch player prepares an offside trap using a free kick.

Individual Tactics

Individual tactics are defined as purposeful, planned, coordinated, offensive and defensive actions a player performs to successfully solve typical game situations, independent of any specific responsibilities related to his position.

The following offensive and defensive actions are performed by an individual player:

Player in Possession of the Ball

- Receiving and moving with the ball.
- Passing.
- Flanking.
- Shot on goal from short and long distances.
- Dribbling to protect ball possession.
- Dribbling for breaking through.

Teammate in Possession of the Ball

- Getting free.
- Being available.

Opposing Player in Possession of the Ball

- Tackling.
- Retreating or delaying.
- Pressuring to the touchline.
- Protecting the goal.
- Coaxing passes towards opponent in vulnerable position.

Opponent Not in Possession of the Ball

- One-on-one coverage.
- Space coverage.

- Coaxing away to prevent pass reception and to intercept passes (see above).
- Interference during ball reception.

Although many of the individual tactical maneuvers were discussed in the chapter on techniques, the emphasis there was on the involvement of the necessary motor skills. Here, tactical skills involved when employing those techniques are discussed.

Individual Offensive Tactics

Receiving and Moving with the Ball

Receiving and driving the ball should always be preceded by a fake. The ball should always be moved into spaces from which effective action can be taken (i.e., a shot on goal, pass, etc.). Faking and moving with the ball can only be accomplished effectively if the player (immediately before he takes possession of the ball) is able to correctly assess his own position, that of his teammates, and that of the opposition.

When receiving the ball, it is important to remember the motto "Body between opponent and ball." This makes it necessary for the player who is about to receive the ball to master ball control with both legs.

Passing

The quality of the pass determines the success of the whole combination play. A pass can be high or flat, hard or soft, with or without spin, and with or without an obvious swinging motion of the leg(s), which announces the direction or type of kick. From the many possibilities, it is clear that,

from a tactical point of view, the type of passing depends on a given game situation.

For passing, the following fundamental rules must be observed:

- Timing, direction, and flight path are determined not by the player who kicks the pass, but by the player who is free to receive the ball. The player who has ball possession must read the movements of his teammates in order to know when and where to direct the pass.
- The type of pass and the type of combination play should be varied constantly during the course of the game. Repeating the same combination makes it easy for the opposition to anticipate and develop tactical countermoves. It is much more difficult to develop countermoves when there is a constant change between through and square passes forward and back passes, long and short passes, and passes kicked directly to a teammate or to an open space.
- Weather and field conditions play a vital role in passing. In heavy mud or deep snow, it is better to kick passes high and wide. On the other hand, smooth, wet grass calls for short, direct passes.
- A pass should be directed to the side of a teammate that is away from the opponent.
- A pass kicked to the forward for a shot on goal should be directed to that player's strong (kicking) foot.

Flanks

Flanks are passes to a receiver that go high above the heads of the opponents or are kicked "blindly" into the dangerous space in front of the opposition's goal.

Tactics and Tactical Training

Basically, the rules are the same as for other passes. However, a few additional points need to be made:

- Flanks with spin are difficult to receive. At the same time, they are more difficult for an opponent to anticipate. With practice, flanks with spin can become very important tactical weapons.
- Corner kicks in the form of flanks kicked with spin towards or away from the goal cause considerable embarrassment for the goalie.
- A shift of game action in midfield should be accomplished exclusively with flanks. This might prevent an interception, if the flank has not been kicked cleanly.
- Flanks directed towards the opposing goal should be short and kicked hard, over the heads of the players. A method used in the past, high-arching passes that drop vertically at the end of the flight, has lost its effectiveness against modern opponents and goalies.

Shots on Goal from Short or Long Distances

Shots on goal from far away create excitement for players and fans alike. These are the shots most likely to be kicked during training. In reality, however, most of the scoring is done from a short distance—within the penalty area. (During the 1988 European Championships, 33 out of 34 goals were scored from there.)

Shots on goal can be made effectively by heading, with the instep or the outside of the instep, and with the inside, tip, or the heel of the foot. The success of a shot depends more on how precisely the ball is kicked than on how hard it is kicked. In addition to technical skills, the player must

possess intuition, good nerves, and lots of tactical routine. From a tactical point of view the following are recommended for shots on goal:

- Shots on goal from a short distance (up to approximately 35 feet (11 m) should be direct, and aimed precisely into the *corner* of the goal box. Aim to avoid the goalpost, *not* the goalkeeper.
- Shots on goal from farther away should be kicked sharply and powerfully and directed to the right or to the left *half* of the goal. Aim at the space between the goalie and the goalpost.
- Shots on goal from a short distance are much more dangerous for the goalie when they come suddenly. For this reason, do not announce your intention with an obvious swing of the kicking leg. Short passes should direct shots on goal, leaving out the "middle man."
- Each goalie has a weak side (usually the left!). Shots on goal to that side obviously have a better chance of being successful.
- Fake the direction and the timing of the kick for shots on goal that follow on the heel of dribbling. The "hidden" kick has a great chance for success. Here, the player kicks while turning, before stopping the dribbling action. The result is that the goalie cannot observe the action or the direction of the shot.
- When shooting in the above-described manner, the position and motions of the goalie have to be taken into consideration. Shots from a narrow angle should be low and with spin. These should be aimed at the long corner.
- If the goalie is relatively far in front of the goal box, he can be

"faked out" by hooking the ball.
- Faking before kicking results in miscalculations on the part of the goalie. The ball can be kicked past him by using the "wrong" foot.
- On smooth, wet grass, low passes, or so-called "bouncing balls," are particularly difficult to calculate.

Methods for Practising Shots on Goal from Short Distances

- Aiming shots towards the goal while running in the penalty area, alternating angles and distances to the goal. The coach stands behind the goal and signals into which corner he wants the shot to go.
- As above, but choosing techniques relevant to the objectives: dribbling, lifting, sharp kicks. The goalie is instructed to change his position in front of and in the goal box.
- As above, but with additional tasks, such as passes that immediately follow a goal. These passes alternate between low and high kicks over short and long distances.
- Game plays of two-on-one, two-on-two, and three-on-three towards the goal. Also, simulating "passing after shots on goal" by using a neutral player for shooting a flank from the side. Two-on-two and three-on-three can be played, switching tasks after the loss of the ball.
- Additional types of plays: one-plus-one on one-plus-one using two small goals; goalie plus two-on-two using small-size goals; goalie plus three-on-three with two neutral players (in the backfield and on the side towards the goal) changing tasks after the loss of the ball; arbi-

trary teams on two goals in half of the playing field with a variety of "provocative" rules (i.e., taboo zones on the sides for the defense, one-time ball contact, scoring only with direct shot on goal, scoring only with heading, etc.).

Dribbling to Keep Possession of the Ball

The following situations are reasons to dribble in order to keep possession of the ball:

- Ballcarrier momentarily does not have a receiver, because his teammates are all covered or are too far away.
- A player moved into offside and passing has to be delayed by dribbling until he is out of the offside position.
- His own team is under heavy pressure; apparently purposeless dribbling in midfield or, even better, in the opposition's half can relieve some of the pressure.

Basic tactical principles for dribbling in order to keep possession of the ball are discussed in the next chapter.

Break-through Dribbling

Break-through dribbling is used in the following situations:

- Counterattack from midfield or defensive move from open space into opponent's territory.
- Countering an opponent's offside trap.
- Taking the risk of dribbling in the opposition's penalty area in order to tempt an opponent to commit a foul and, thereby, gain a penalty kick for the team.

All three methods of dribbling ask players to keep in mind several points:

- Do not start dribbling from a standing position; start from a running position.
- Always start dribbling with a fake.
- In principle, the player should always observe his opponent while dribbling.

Decisiveness and enthusiasm are written all over the dribbler's face.

Tactics and Tactical Training

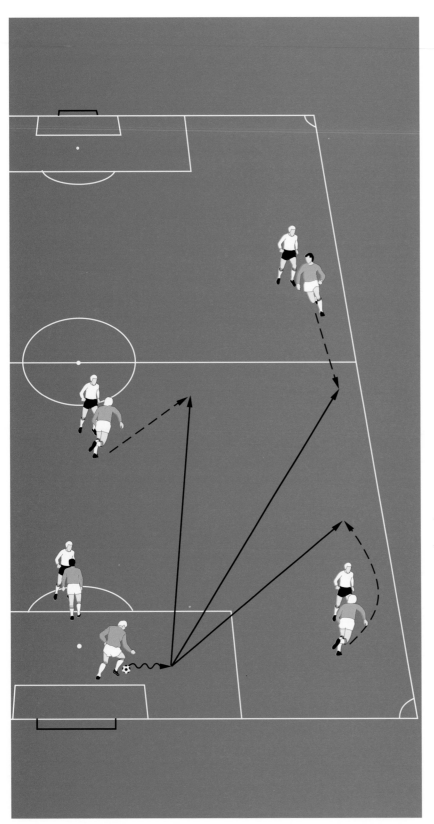

Getting Free and Being Available

In general, a player gets free in order to become available to receive a pass; however, there are other reasons for getting free:

- To exchange positions with a teammate (wide change).
- To make room for a teammate for break-through dribbling (deep change).
- To lure a player away from a one-on-one coverage, creating a hole in the defense of the opposition.
- To fake a particular combination and facilitate the surprise action of a teammate.

Running to get free requires the player to pay attention to the following:

Timing

Running should commence at the moment a teammate has given the signal (by eye contact) that he is ready to pass. If he starts too early, he might be covered again before the pass has been kicked; if too late, the opposing player has the advantage when he tackles. Proper timing is particularly important when playing direct combinations. For newly formed teams or new groups or pairs (i.e., midfielder passing/forward getting free and receiving), it often takes weeks or months until the necessary fine-tuning of time and space is in place. Also, for the same reason, it takes time to integrate a new player into the team.

Getting free within one's own defensive zone.

Tactics and Tactical Training

The Form

Getting free is accomplished with a sudden start, or better yet, with fake steps to the right for a start to the left, and vice versa. The player should attempt to run behind his opponent so that the opponent cannot observe him and the ball at the same time.

Direction

This question is especially difficult to answer, because for each of the countless game situations there are several effective possibilities. Sepp Herberger stated 50 years ago: "Go to the man with the ball," and demanded at the same time: "A player must also be able to stay away." This is still true today. The following basic rules make "getting free" more interesting and more difficult for the opponent to read:

● When in his own half of the field, a player makes himself available by running towards the touchline.

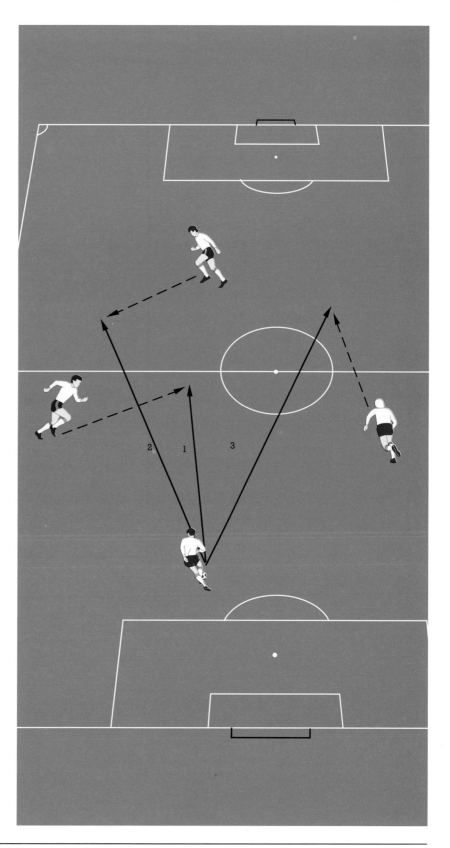

Getting free by running a diagonal pattern.

Tactics and Tactical Training

- In midfield, the player runs a diagonal pattern, trying to get behind the opponent.
- The movement of the center forward depends on the position of the sweeper and the distance to the goal. Also, the offside limit must be watched. The forward, therefore, often has to run at right angles or diagonally back to his own midfield area to get free.

- If several players are running to get free at the same time, actions should be coordinated in such a way that the ballcarrier has the choice of passing in every direction.

Here is the ideal situation: The player in possession of the ball has the option of passing in all directions.

The forward can run either wide or deep to get free.

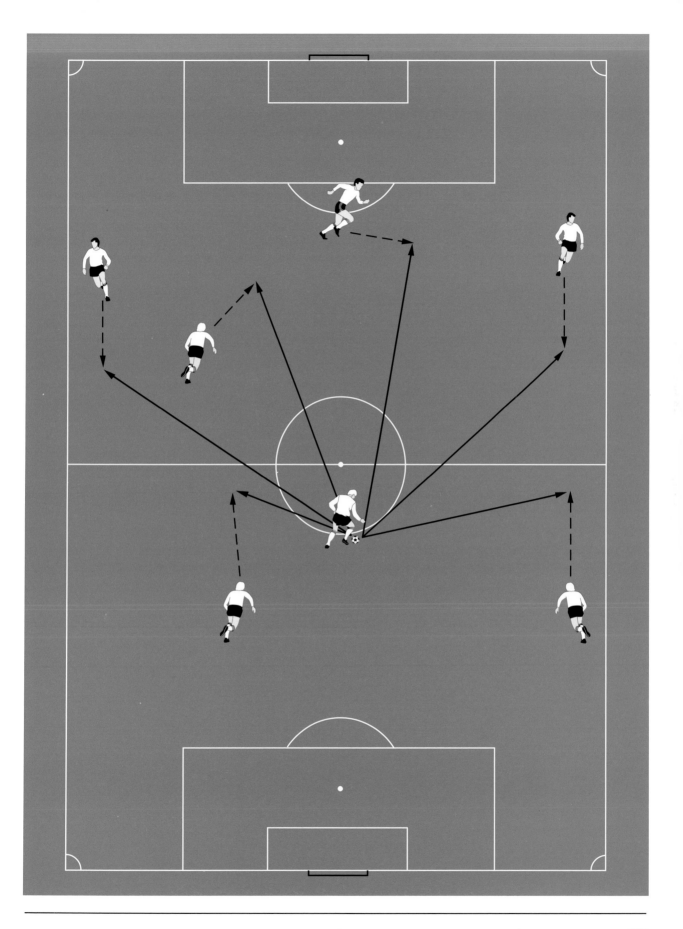

Tactics and Tactical Training

Individual Defensive Tactics

Tackling

A player well trained in tactics does not tackle *at the first possible moment*, but *at the best possible moment*. The following "moments" are best suited to take the ball away from the opponent:

- The very moment when the opponent is trying to receive the ball. The player covering the intended receiver jumps decisively in front of him, either taking control of the ball or kicking the ball away from the opponent.
- The moment the receiver is trying to take possession and move away with the ball. At this point, he is standing on one leg and is totally involved in starting to pass, leaving him little opportunity to defend himself.
- When the opponent is already in possession of the ball. Wait for the moment when he briefly lets the ball bounce off his foot.

The last situation is not quite as favorable. The defensive player must turn the situation to his advantage with additional tactics. It is important that he:

- Match the tempo of the opponent 6 to 10 feet (2–3 m) away from him.
- Not approach the opponent from the front but from the side. In this way he has totally blocked the opponent's move to one side and is pushing him in the direction of his own, stronger leg.
- With a fake, lure the opponent into a miscalculation, creating a favorable situation for either a hook or a slide tackle.

It is important that a hook or a slide tackle only be considered when the player is totally sure of his success. If not, the dribbler will be difficult to catch, since the player must first get back on his feet, before he can pursue the opponent again.

Moving Back and Delaying

If a team is outnumbered by the opposition, as the members move from midfield in the direction of the goal, the attack on the ball-carrying player must be delayed. While one player continues to engage the ballcarrier, the rest of the defense covers the opposing players until reinforcements arrive from midfield and the numerical balance is reestablished.

Defenders should always attack in such a way that a pass to the opposing forward, whose position creates the greatest danger (usually the center forward), is blocked. While the defender is moving back, he does not let up on his attack on the ballcarrier, preventing him from making a successful pass.

Dribbling and tackling are basic elements of the game.

If the opposition outnumbers the defense, the attack must be delayed; at the same time, the pass to an opponent is blocked.

Pushing to the Side

This tactic has already been mentioned in the chapter on tackling. If a defender in midfield sees no chance to successfully tackle the ball-carrying opponent, he should at least try to prevent the dribbler from breaking through in the direction of the goal. Here, the opponent is given room on the side of his strong kicking leg, while he is constantly pushed in the direction of the touchline.

Protecting the Goal

If a player in possession of the ball is dangerously close to the goal, it is more important to block a possible shot on goal than to try to gain ball possession, which might be faster, but is very risky. In this case, the defender moves between the ball and the player in such a way that he can block the stronger kicking leg of the opponent. He is then forced to dribble with his weaker leg or to kick a square or back pass. This gives other teammates an opportunity to regain ball control.

Tactics and Tactical Training

Protection Against Dangerous Passes

What we have discussed above is also true in protecting against dangerous passes. For instance, when an opponent has gained ball control in his own half of the field, he will quickly try to switch from defense to offense. He will usually have only one or two (and for the opponent very dangerous) possibilities for passing. The attacking player should position himself at least in such a way that the opponent is unable to pass accurately. An aggressive attack to regain the ball can only be made when the particularly dangerous opponent is again covered.

One-on-One Coverage

One-on-one coverage is also called opponent-centered coverage. Usually a defender concentrates on one particular player. He can either cover him closely (press-cover) or lightly—6 to 10 feet (3–5 m) away.

Close coverage means actual body contact. It is more difficult for the offensive player to lose the defender when only a narrow space remains between the two players. Basically, a defender should choose a position that enables him to:
• Stand between the opponent and his own goal.
• Keep his eyes on the opponent and the ball.
• Stand on the side that is closest to the ball, diagonally behind the opponent.

Covering In-between Space

An individual player only takes over space coverage when his teammates are outnumbered. Here, a player positions himself between two opponents, keeping his eyes on both. The opponent who is closest to the ball and the goal must be covered tightly. If the ball is passed to one of the two opponents, the one who is the likely receiver is attacked with one-on-one coverage.

The position of the defenders in one-on-one coverage depends on the game situation and where the ball is. The sweeper stands on the side closest to the ball in the back.

Tactics and Tactical Training

Game Positions and Tactics

In the section on individual tactics, we talked about the tasks of an individual player and the tactics he can use to solve specific game situations. This, generally, applies to all players, regardless of their position. Depending on his specific position, each player has additional tasks and special tactics at his disposal.

Defensive and offensive tactics depend very much on the tactics of the group or team. In reverse, the sum of the tactical methods that are specific to one individual position influence the complex whole. Therefore, if a coach is primarily oriented towards group and team tactics at the expense of individual tactics, he is doomed from the start.

Tactics and the Goalkeeper

The tactics used by a goalie are markedly different from any other player. One look at the rules of the game makes it clear that the goalie occupies a special position within the team, with tactics specifically designed for his position. The following aspects of the tactics of a goalkeeper are particularly important:

- How he positions himself in the box and in front of the goal.
- His basic position during shots on goal.
- Catching and/or punching.
- Handling the ball from a dribbling forward.
- Handling offensive action.
- Handling defensive action.

- How he handles the penalty kick.
- Building a "wall" against a free kick.

Position In and in Front of the Goal Box

The goalkeeper's position is influenced by his ability to orient himself not only in the box but also in the penalty area. Because the game is constantly changing, a goalkeeper is always on the move, following the flight direction of the ball. When moving out of the box, he has to defend the empty goal box behind him (when the ball is coming towards the center of the goal), the space to the right (when attacked from the right), and the space to the left (when the attack comes from the left). He must always get back to the center of the goal. Since he is concentrating on the ball, he must orient himself spatially in the box and the pen-

alty area. To help do this, many goalkeepers draw an additional vertical line through the middle of the goal box towards the playing field (which is unlawful).

Standard situations, like free kicks and corner kicks, are particularly difficult for the goalie when the penalty area is crowded. Often he has only fractions of a second to make the decision to leave the box.

Basic Position for Shots on Goal

Some goalkeepers belong to the category of "fliers." They often make spectacular leaps to compensate for their lack of positioning skills. A good goalie is always at the right place at the right time intuitively; which is to say, he is always in the position from which he has the best possible chance for an effective defense.

The center is the best of all possible places for a goalkeeper.

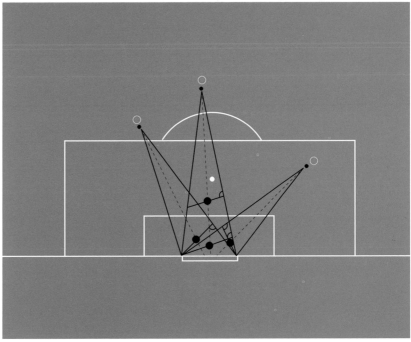

Tactics and Tactical Training

Distance of the Ball from the Goal

Here are the basic rules:

- If the ball is in the opposition's half of the field, the goalie steps up to the edge of the penalty area, in order to catch a possible through ball.
- If the ball is in his half of the field, up to about 75 feet (25 m) in front of the goal, he remains on the line so as not to be surprised by wide passes with descending curves.
- If an opponent approaches with the ball and reaches the penalty area, the goalie runs towards him in such a way that he shortens the angle of approach. Note: Whenever a goalie leaves the goal box, he should shift the point of gravity of his body forward to the balls of his feet. He can react most quickly from such a position.

The Angle of the Ball's Flight Path and the Direction from Which the Opponent Approaches the Goal

The rules are as follows:

- If the opponent approaches the goal, and the space in which he can effectively make his shot on goal is a section with a 45-degree spread, the goalie takes a position as shown in the drawing on page 119.
- If the opponent approaches at a sharp angle, the goalie moves slightly back in the direction of the goal line at an angle about half the above number. From this position, he is better able to control balls with spin that are kicked into the long corner. This position is also better for incoming flanks and back passes.

The Position of His Own Defensive Player

The following basic rules apply:

- As long as a teammate is involved in a one-on-one with a ball-carrying opponent, the goalie remains in his basic position in the goal box.
- If a teammate is covering part of the goal, the goalie can move towards the "unprotected" area of the goal, safeguarding that space.

Catching and Punching

When the opposition attacks from the side with corner kicks and flanks, the goalie often has to make decisions with lightning speed: to catch or to punch the high, incoming ball. The following basic rules apply:

- Balls that can be handled confidently and securely should be caught.
- When the ground and the ball are wet, or when in doubt, punching is preferred to catching.
- Since the reach with one arm is greater than with both, balls that can barely be reached should be punched; this also applies to shots on goal that can be deflected on the line.
- Balls that are kicked into the penalty area from the right should be punched away from the penalty area to the left side with the right hand, and vice versa. A variation of punching with the fist is to use the flat of the hand. This extends the goalie's reach, allowing him to push a high pass over the horizontal board or a low pass into a corner around the goalpost.

Leaping

As has already been mentioned, a goalkeeper is seldom forced to leap, if he knows how to properly position himself. If it should be necessary, the leap should be preceded by a short step. A leap to the right begins by moving the left leg in front of the right pivot leg in the direction of the leap. One step with the right leg begins the jumping move.

Goalkeeper and Penalty Kicks

The referee's whistle is the signal for the goalie to start his tactical maneuver. On principle, the goalie should never get involved in the discussion over the decision itself. The calmer he remains, the more he will impress the player who makes the shot. When playing in league soccer, where the player making the penalty kick is well known, it is good for the goalie to keep written notes about past penalty kicks.

For the shot itself, the goalie must concentrate only on the ball and the foot of the shooter. They will give him information about the corner chosen for the shot. The shooter will try using fakes to irritate the goalie; likewise, the goalie can deceive the shooter with fake movements of his upper body and by swinging his arms back and forth. Blind and often premature leaps towards a particular corner of the box usually are not successful. For teams playing in lower divisions, who have weaker penalty shooters, it makes more sense to expect a less accurately kicked ball. The goalie should calmly remain in the middle, expecting the ball to come from either the left or the right side.

The "Wall" as Defense Against a Free Kick

A well-positioned "wall" can greatly decrease the danger of a

Tactics and Tactical Training

free kick. Opinions over who should position the wall are divided. It can be the player who stands immediately behind the ball and can look over the ball in the direction of the goalpost on the near side. Most goalkeepers, however, want to arrange the wall themselves. To do so, they must leave the prime space in the middle of the box, which may, when the free kick is executed quickly, give the opposition a chance to score.

The directions from the goalie must be loud, clear, and distinct. It is best to use the names of the respective players who are posted at the outside of the wall. The list must be recited with a calm voice. Basically, the wall is posted approximately two feet (½ m) beyond the direct line between the ball and the goalpost.

The Goalkeeper and Defense

Usually the goalie is regarded as the key person on a team. He should take advantage of this role and direct the defense from the rear. If he pays close attention to the game he, better than anyone else, is able to detect weaknesses in the defensive coverage of an in-dividual player, of a group, and of the opposing team. If the goalkeeper and the defense communicate well, then all that is needed is calling the name of the individual whose coverage is not quite up to par.

The Goalkeeper and Offense

The goalie should be the number-one offensive player on the team.

Passes to a forward should be kicked so that they hit the ground about 15 feet (5 m) in front of him. The flight path of a bouncing ball is easier to handle for the forward than for the defender behind him.

A penalty kick, the dramatic end of an exciting game. The goalie stands in the center.

Tactics and Tactical Training

Tactics of the Sweeper

The tasks of the sweeper are as follows:

Directing the Defense

Because of his position on the field, the sweeper has a good view of the developments of a game; from this position he can guide the movements and actions of his teammates.

Safeguarding the Front Line

This tactic was already mentioned in the section on group tactics (see page 105). The sweeper usually moves with the ball. If one of his teammates is trying to regain ball possession with a one-on-one, the sweeper will provide cover. The distance between the sweeper and the opponent narrows as the opponent approaches the goal. Ideally, he will be no more than 6 to 10 feet (2 to 3 m) behind the defender.

Safeguarding Open Space and Lanes

Passes are not only kicked to covered forwards, but also into open lanes and spaces. Since the sweeper does not have an opponent he is directly responsible for, he is free to cover open spaces and is, therefore, an ideal receiver. Experienced sweepers leave lanes open on purpose (or as a provocation) in order to facilitate a pass to the open space. With experience and a good eye, he is usually able to intercept the pass.

Passing as a Signal to Initiate Offense

Due to his position on the field, the sweeper often has the best chance to initiate offensive action without interference. Time and again, the sweeper receives short passes from his teammates. Depending on the situation, he uses them for short or long offensive passes.

Joining the Offensive Line

The modern sweeper actively participates in the offensive action. Sometimes he does this to bring an element of surprise into the game; sometimes, because his team is trailing. Since he does not have a designated opponent, he is able to move far into the territory of the opposition before he is attacked. Ideally, the penetration into the opposition's territory should be on the side where the opposing forward is restricted in his actions (because he is covering *his* opponent) or where the opposition has obvious weaknesses.

Sometimes, the sweeper is part of the four-man defensive line as a second inside defender. Oftentimes, the two inside defenders switch back and forth in their tasks of covering open space. This only makes sense in a four-man defensive line. In a 3–5–2 system, the sweeper must, among other things, alternate between the open spaces on the left and the right of both defenders.

Tactics of the Defenders

The action of a defender in one-on-one coverage or space coverage depends on the team's tactics (see page 94). There is a marked difference between the tactics of the inside defender and the outside defender. For instance, the inside defender primarily attacks the center forward in the middle of the field in front of his own goal. This function is so vital that he seldom will get involved in his team's offensive actions or take over other defensive tasks.

Not so the outside defender. He will switch from his designated position in the direction of the goal, if the ball is played on the opposite side of the field, so that he can support the sweeper in covering the dangerous space in front of the goal. It is OK to leave the coverage of his direct opponent, because if the ball returns to his side, he has enough time to get back to the opponent for whom he is responsible.

Modern outside defenders get involved in the offensive game of their teams along the touchlines much earlier than in the past. This is particularly effective when the opposition plays with only three defenders (the 3–5–2 system), or if the defender's own outside forward (through a change in midfield) lures the opposing defender to the touchline. The attack of the defender can take place either as a counterattack or as a frontal attack.

Basically, the defender should finish his attack with positive actions (flanks or shots on goal) and not get involved in a risky dribbling action that might cost him the ball.

Tactics of the Midfielders

To a certain degree, every midfielder has offensive and defensive tasks to fulfill. These players are responsible for switching quickly from offense to defense and from defense to offense.

In addition, they are involved in the shifting action from one side of the field to the other. Changing the rhythm of the game is also their responsibility (see page 91). Teams that play with four or more midfielders often pair them up. Only one of the two pairs may get involved at any one time in an offensive action.

Action zones for midfielders can, as has already been mentioned, vary widely. Some of the examples are shown on page 118. During fast counterattacks, midfielders should choose diagonal running patterns. Usually these players should move at the edges of the defensive zones—an elegant way of avoiding the attacks of opposing players. Continuous diagonal running patterns make it difficult for the opposing sweeper to maintain position and game strategy. The modern midfielder must have the skills of a forward. The following are expected of him:

- Moving the ball in dynamic fashion into the territory of the opposition.
- Covering long distances in open space to reach the sides (wings).
- From that position, using flanks and back passes to the defense line.
- With long passes from the second line, forcing a defensively oriented opposition to attack prematurely.

Tactics of the Center Forward

Today's center forwards are often left to their own devices, while being outnumbered by the opposing defense. Most of the time they are brought into the action because of a through pass. They must hold

A shot on goal is the spice of the game. Intuition and tactical skills are closely connected.

their own against a great number of defensive players or control the ball until midfield players can move up for support. In both cases, the task can only be accomplished if they have great technical skills and can control a ball with *both* legs. They can evade direct, tight coverage by changing positions and pulling to the outside. To balance the disadvantage of being outnumbered, one of the two center forwards can move in the direction of the sweeper. In this way, a forward ties up both the defender and the sweeper in a small space. This tactic clears space for a breakaway by the midfielder, who is moving upfield.

Teams that play with two center forwards can create havoc in the defense with the following tactics:

Position Change of Center Forwards—from left to right or from right to left, immediately ini-

tiating a combination play.

Position Change in Open Space—Here, one player starts to move on an angle towards the rear; the other player moves on a forward angle so that the teammate in midfield has the possibility of passing either wide or short.

Giving Over and Luring Away—In a small space immediately in front of the goal, the dribbling center forward can give the ball over to the teammate next to him, at the same time luring away an attacking opponent.

Position Change for Receiving a Flank—To prepare for flanks, the center forwards run diagonally across the field, crossing each other as each heads for one of the goalposts. Short passes are handled by the player at the short side of the goal, long passes by the other player.

Tactics and Tactical Training

Tactics of a Standard Situation

Between 20 and 30 percent of all goals scored are the result of standard situations. For this reason, they should be intensely studied and practised during training.

Teams that use their technical skills and physical strength well in standard situations (i.e., throw-in far into the penalty area) will have many advantages. Standard situations are divided into the following:

- The tactics of the attacker in possession of the ball.
- The tactics of the defending team.

Offensive players have the tactical advantage because they can bring the ball into play without being pressured by the opposition and without any immediate time pressure. Sadly, not enough use is made of this advantage.

The kickoff at the start of the first half serves to keep control of the ball.

Tactics for Kickoff

Offense Kickoff Tactics

The situation for the team that is kicking off depends on whether the kickoff is at the start of the game or period or after the opposition has scored. At the *beginning of a period* and after the first ball has been kicked forward (as required by the rules), the ball should be immediately passed back. Driving the ball to the opposition's half is not good tactics because of the great number of players present there. The back pass lures the opposition out of its half of the field, changing the balance to its disadvantage. In addition, the back pass gives teammates the opportunity to lose their initial nervousness by getting involved in unpressured combination plays.

For psychological reasons, the kickoff *after a successful score by the opposition* is totally different. The opposition is ecstatic. The players are so busy congratulating themselves that they don't concentrate on the kickoff. The "excited bunch" hasn't quite dissolved when the kickoff takes place, and the defensive players are not yet in their proper positions. In such a situation, the kickoff should be a counterattack. The ball is driven with quick through passes into the open space where the opposition has not yet taken up coverage. A precision flank kicked to the forward, sprinting after tempo dribbling has moved the ball to the touchline, is particularly effective.

The surprise counterattack kickoff after a successful score by the opposition.

Tactics and Tactical Training

Defensive Kickoff Tactics

The variations discussed so far make it clear how important it is that every player concentrate on the defense when the opposition kicks off. The defensive team should not give away its tactical advantage (the concentration of manpower in its half of the field) and move too many players forward too quickly. It is sufficient to move two or three players into the territory of the opposition and to start pressing the man who has the ball.

Both center forwards (positioned at the line between the kickoff circle while the midline opposition kicks off) have a good chance to intercept the back pass. They must sprint aggressively into enemy territory while the kickoff is carried out. The opposition seldom counts on such actions. The surprise often causes them to lose the ball after the first few contacts.

A tactic for quick recovery of the ball after the opposition's kickoff: Both center forwards immediately start towards the opposition's half of the field in order to intercept the back pass.

Tactics and Tactical Training

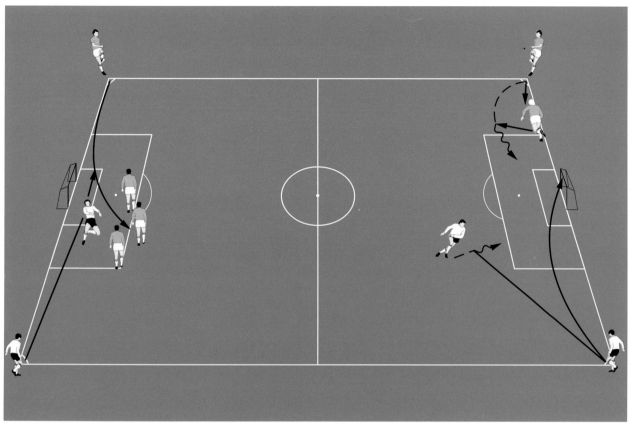

Four different possibilities for corner kicks.

Tactics for Corner Kicks

Offensive Tactics and Corner Kicks

The offensive tactics used in case of a corner kick and the position of the attacking players depend on the following factors:

- Strength and ability of the players (for instance, a strong corner kicker, expert shooters from the second line, a dribbling expert).
- Strength and ability of the opposition (for instance, goalkeeper with good ball control in the penalty area, tall players with good heading skills).
- Outside conditions (such as sun, wind, and ground condition).
  Basically, the offensive strategy

for corner kicks is governed by the following:

- The more players there are in the goal area, the more difficult it is for the goalkeeper to field the ball outside the goal box. For this reason, it is prudent to have at least two attackers in this area to act as troublemakers, even if they don't have good heading skills.
- Corner kicks that spin towards the goal or away from it are difficult for the goalie to judge.
- Sharp, straight corner kicks are more difficult to handle by the defense than balls that are curving.
- It is easy for the opposition to adapt to corner kicks that are always made in the same fashion; therefore, use several variations.

It is recommended that the corner kicker signal his teammates so that they are aware of the type of kick he intends to make.
  What follows are a few variations that have proven to be effective.

Long Corner Kick

This ball, kicked with spin, moves away from the goal towards the goalpost at the far end, between the penalty area and the goal area.

Corner Kick to the Near Corner of the Goal Area

Here, the ball is sharply kicked to the inside at head level. This method is recommended if the opposition as a whole is good at heading.

Tactics and Tactical Training

Short Corner Kick

The ball is passed to a teammate positioned only a short distance away. The teammate should move as quickly as possible along the goal line into the penalty area. When this maneuver is used, it is important to make sure that the opposition (after the first pass) is not given a chance to set an off-side trap. This method has the advantage over other corner-kick methods in that the team keeps ball possession. The short corner kick is also recommended if the team has a good dribbler, who can drive the ball decisively into the opposition's penalty area.

This is the basic defensive position of a team.

Corner Kick as Back Pass

Here, the ball is moved back, deep into midfield, where the team can control ball possession, or the corner kick can be concluded by an expert attempting a shot on goal from the second line. This method is particularly good in the last moments of a game, when the team has a narrow lead. Controlling the ball in midfield, as well as shooting from the second line, gains valuable time and might save the game.

Corner Kick and Defensive Tactics

The defensive team can make up for the tactical advantage of the attacker with the following actions:

Safeguarding the Goal Area and the Goalkeeper

This is accomplished with one or two defenders. One is positioned directly in the goal area next to or near the goalpost (so as not to obstruct the goalie's view); the second defender is positioned at the goalpost at the far end. If the goalie has to leave the box to intercept a flank, both defenders move to the middle of the goal area, protecting both halves.

Safeguarding the Goal

Experience has shown that during corner-kick action, most scoring is the result of headers by players who are positioned just inside or outside of the goal line.

Therefore, the front of the goal line should be safeguarded by three defensive players. If the corner kick comes into the goal area, these players can cover the goalie; if the ball comes into the portion of the penalty area in front of the line, the defenders have a good chance to move the ball to midfield.

Preventing Corner Kicks

Often a defensive player moves within 30 feet (9 m) of the corner-kick area in order to prevent the shooter from kicking accurately and to interfere with a possible short corner kick.

Guarding Strong Opposing Headers

Strong headers of the opposing team are usually discovered early in the game. When, in the course of a corner-kick action, tall defensive players leave their position and move forward, trouble lies ahead. These players must be covered by teammates who are equally strong headers. But they must not be deceived by fake kicking motions prior to the corner kick, which might lead to mistaken responses. Whenever the opponent jumps in the air for a header, the defending player must follow his movements, even if there is no chance of reaching the ball. This is the only way to prevent dangerous headers.

Constructing an Offside Trap

A successful defense of the first corner kick does not mean that all danger has passed. If the ball has been kicked out of the penalty area to the feet of an opponent, it is imperative that this opponent immediately be attacked by two defensive players simultaneously. This attack is the signal for the

Because the chance for success is so great, the corner kick always creates high tension for the players and fans alike.

whole team to move forward with lightning speed, because it moves the offside line away from the dangerous goal area.

Initiating Counterattacks

The opponent usually gives up his regular defensive positions during corner kicks. The opposition has only a few players in its half of the field. This is an ideal situation in which to initiate assault-like counterattacks. The attack can be started by the goalie after he has fielded the ball. A punt deep into the enemy's territory is particularly good. A well-aimed throw to

either of the two players who are waiting at the left and right corners of the penalty area can also initiate a quick attack.

Basic Position of Defending Players

The type of corner kick the opposition has planned is usually not known. Therefore, the defending team must choose positions from which every defensive tactic discussed so far can be successfully carried out (compare drawing, page 128).

Tactics and Tactical Training

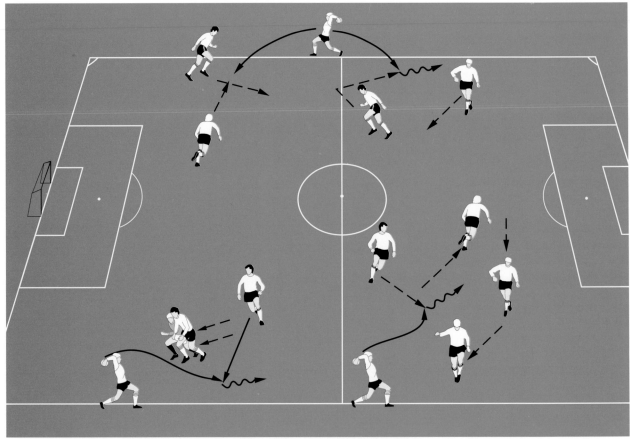

Good coordination allows a team to use many different methods for the throw-in. Here are four examples.

Tactics for a Throw-In

Offensive Tactics

The requirements for the throw-in are the same as those for combination plays:

- One or two players get free at the same time.
- The free players, who have switched positions, open space for each other by taking their direct cover with them into another zone (see drawing above).
- The players who are free determine the type, time, and direction of the throw-in.
- In contrast to regular combination plays, the offside rule is sus-

pended during a throw-in. This allows the players who are free to run behind the opposing defense. This is also a way to avoid a concentration of opposing defenders gathering around the throw-in.
- The direction of the throw-in depends on the place from which it is made. In general, we distinguish between four different situations:

Throw-in Deep in the Team's Own Territory

In order to avoid square passes in front of the team's own goal, the throw-in should always be made

forward along the touchlines (see drawing above). Under no circumstances should a square pass move the ball into the middle of the team's own territory.

Midfield Throw-in—Opponent Attacking

The sweeper gets free by running in the direction of the player throwing the ball; a midfielder starts to run behind the waiting players' backs into the free space (see drawing above).

Midfield Throw-in—Opponent Defending

The midfielder, positioned across the field from the opponent throw-

Tactics and Tactical Training

.ng the ball, begins to move forward, taking his cover with him. Defenders or midfield players, coming from behind, get free by running into the free space (see drawing).

Throw-in in Front of the Opponent's Goal

Because of the suspension of the offside rule during throw-ins, the sweepers are able to move all the way into the goal area. Immediately before the throw-in, midfield players run towards the penalty area. The ball is thrown in the direction of the penalty area. At the same time, the midfielders move forward and try to intercept the throw-in.

Throw-in and Defensive Tactics

Defensive players move according to the same guidelines that we have discussed for combination plays. This means that the defenders are tightly covered in the immediate area of the ball, and their movements are followed with one-on-one coverage. In addition, it is important that the opposing defenders, who are farther away, do not move freely behind the offside line.

Tactics for the Free Kick

Free Kick and Offensive Tactics

According to the rules, free kicks can be kicked *directly* or *indirectly*.

For free kicks *in midfield*, a team should make good use of the basic tactical advantage, possession of the ball. To do so, the team keeps control of the ball in its own territory by kicking short, sure, quick passes back and forth. Because of the danger of losing the ball, through passes are seldom called for.

Well-trained teams have a large repertoire of methods for free kicks. Here are four examples of the many possibilities.

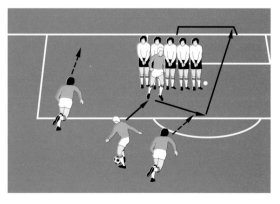

Tactics and Tactical Training

A clever free kick can overcome a well-constructed "wall."

Many different methods are available for free kicks *close to the goal of the opposition.* A free kick can be executed quickly, surprising the opponent, but only after the referee has returned the ball. If a quick free kick is not possible, the kick should be carefully planned. The following possibilities are available:

Direct Shot on Goal

Each team has players who are able to turn their shooting strength into dangerous free-kick weapons. Well-aimed balls that are kicked sharply with spin (around the "wall" or over the wall into either of the corners of the goal) are particularly dangerous for the goalkeeper, since it is difficult to anticipate the direction of the ball.

Indirect Shot on Goal

Three attackers are needed to accomplish the indirect free kick: one player for the free kick and two other players, one to his left and one to his right. This basic strategy can be varied in many ways. It is an easy method to deceive the opposition. Several examples are shown in the drawings. Regardless of which variation is chosen, a few players should be positioned to the left and right of the opponent's wall. Their presence obstructs the goalie's view even more.

Free Kick and Defensive Tactics

Free kicks by the opposition can be successfully defended if every member of the team is involved. Each player has a clearly defined role. Players should take their positions as quickly as possible but with absolute calmness. The sequence of movements must be planned, and the strategy must be practised during training until it becomes almost automatic.

- The player closest to the ball takes a position a few yards away to prevent a quick, direct kick. At the same time, the "wall" is assembled with the assigned players. The tallest players are posted at the corners.
- The goalkeeper or one of the players (usually the one positioned behind the ball) gives clear, concise instructions.
- The rest of the players assume coverage of the space to the right and left of the wall.

In case of an indirect free kick, the wall should move (after the first contact with the ball) forward to shorten the angle or suddenly dissolve, allowing the players to switch to one-on-one coverage.

Free Kicks from a Narrow Angle

Free kicks between the penalty area and the touchlines are particularly dangerous, because they can be aimed at the area immediately in front of the goal. For this reason, a wall of at least three defenders is recommended. The formation of the rest of the players is the same as for the basic corner kick (see drawing).

Tactics and Tactical Training

Tactics for Penalty Kicks

Penalty Kick—Offensive and Defensive Tactics

A penalty kick is awarded when a foul, that otherwise would have resulted in a free kick, is committed within the penalty area. Indirect penalty kicks are possible, but seldom awarded. In the case of an indirect penalty kick, the ball must be played forward.

The offside rule is in effect during the penalty kick. Therefore, the offensive player may not be closer to the opposition's goal line than the last defending opponent. This is the only position from which players can reach for a ball that is bouncing off a goalpost or is punched out by the goalkeeper without running into an offside situation.

A basic, logical formation for offensive and defensive players is shown in the drawings. Players of both teams line up along the penalty area so that the bouncing ball can be handled equally well by defenders and attackers.

Training for Standard Situations

The above discussion makes it clear that standard situations give a team numerous possibilities for intelligent tactical maneuvers.

Combining theory with systematic, practical exercises of game situations will improve the tactical skills of individual players and the team as a whole. This holds true for both defensive and offensive players.

Many coaches shy away from practising standard situations, because they believe that players do not get enough physical conditioning in the process. This is only partly true. Training for standard situations can be planned separately, before or after regular practice sessions.

Because of the lighter training load, such training can be scheduled more frequently after the second half of the competitive period. Since games become more important in the second half of the season, tactical skills for standard situations become especially important.

The basic formation of attackers and defenders for a penalty kick.

Tactics and Tactical Training

Tactics for the Day

The tactics employed by a team, group of players, and individual players need to be adjusted according to the specific conditions of the day.

The components of the tactics used by the team and the individual players have already been reviewed on page 86. We will examine few aspects in more detail.

Long-term Goal and Standings

The long-term goal for the team is defined by management (in the case of professional teams), the coach, and the team. The actual tactical maneuvers to be used are influenced by the team's standing in the division and the overall team objectives. For instance, if a team has planned to advance to a higher standing in its respective division during the next two or three years, and if the desired level has already been reached for the current season, the tactics will clearly be different (more risky, more aggressive) than when the team was in last place.

Actual Objectives for the Day

For amateur teams and teams with young players, the objective of every game ought to be to win—with as wide a margin as possible. With that expectation, tactics are clearly defined.

From European championship games, we know that for professional soccer teams, even a narrow loss (in point games) is sufficient for the team's advancement. In this case, defensive tactics are the

choice. Defensive specialists will see more action, the game system will be different, the defenders must play a much more disciplined defense, and so forth.

Actual Condition of the Team

The actual performance level of the team varies for many different reasons. Players are injured, suspended, or in a personal slump; new players have to be integrated into the team; a winning or losing streak has lifted or depressed the mood, and conflicts within the team have undermined the willingness to perform.

These factors must be recognized by the coach and the lineup (see also page 15), and the choice of tactics must reflect these conditions.

The Opposing Team

We know of very few games in which a team is so superior that it can rightfully say, "What do I care about the opponent? He has to play our game!" It is *always* important to find out as much as possible about the opposition. They, too, can have a bad day for the same reasons pointed out above. It is difficult to plan ahead for such a situation. However, many factors that can influence a game are often known or can be anticipated. These can and should influence the tactics the team wants to use.

Through close observation, a good coach will gain important information early in the game. This information can be passed on to his players in the form of tips and calls during the game or at halftime. In order to make an immedi-

ate analysis of the opposition, the following points are important:
● Lineup.
● Game system.
● Group and team tactics.
● Specific variations of standard situations.
● Particularly strong or weak players.
● Overall physical condition of individual players.

Type of Game

Although soccer players play to win, the type of game a team is playing (training, friendship, point, or championship) will influence how a win, a tie, or a loss is evaluated. A loss in a point game can be made up in the next game; in a championship game, a loss means the team is out. It is clear that these factors influence the choice of tactics.

Training and friendship games are good times to experiment with different methods and lineups. The final score is not very important.

Day and Time of the Game

Teams playing a Friday–Wednesday–Friday schedule often try to reserve the necessary energy for the next match by playing a calm, ball-controlling type of game. Teams with good technical skills have an advantage in such a situation.

Games played under the lights, as compared to day games, require different considerations. For instance:

● Players who wear glasses are at a disadvantage, and that has consequences for the lineup

Tactics and Tactical Training

- Dark uniforms are difficult to make out. If need be, the team has to wear different uniforms, replacing their favorite team jerseys or shorts with others.
- Because of the lights, balls kicked high in the air are difficult for all players to judge, but especially so for the opposing goalkeeper.

Location of the Game

Tactics are often different for games played at home than for those played away from home. Location can even influence the game system. Many teams play more defensively when on the road than they do in front of their own fans. Sometimes, at an away game, a coach hopes that the opposition, in the euphoria of playing in front of its fans, will get a little bit careless. This makes counterattacking much easier.

Also, games played in other countries, particularly those with an unfamiliar climate, require special tactics and considerations. This also holds true for pre-game preparations (overnight accommodations, nutrition, fluids necessary for the climate, and medical care, such as inoculations).

Other Conditions

Conditions change from day to day and from game to game. It is possible to adjust tactics with the following in mind:

- Climate and weather.
- Playing field and ground conditions.
- Fans.
- Referee.

Climate and Weather

Very high temperatures require special preparation (proper fluids) and influence the choice of tactics (for instance, using combinations that force the opposition to do most of the running).

During the winter months, the choice of proper clothing is important (gloves and tights).

Actual weather conditions, such as rain, the angle of the sun, and wind direction and velocity, play an important role. It makes sense to choose the half in which the team can play with the wind and the sun at its back, even though those conditions might change during the course of the game. When playing against the wind, it is a good idea to use low passes and to drive the ball forward with safe, combination plays.

Condition of Playing Field and the Ground

Dimensions of playing fields vary greatly, especially in amateur and youth leagues. The same is true of the condition of the ground (grass, ash, artificial grass, snow, and mud). These conditions are different from field to field and even within a field. These variations have to be considered when choosing shoes. They will also influence the way the game is played. For instance, wet grass calls for short passes and accurate kicking; in muddy conditions and in deep snow, however, passes must be high and wide.

Expectations of the Fans

The expectations and reactions of fans is different in different places; professional players ought to adjust the type of game they want to play accordingly.

The Referee

In spite of the fact that all referees receive the same training, their interpretation of rules is not the same every time. This is particularly true of Rule #12. Smart players adjust their behavior on the field and their one-on-one confrontations accordingly.

Personal Goals

A solid performance for the good of the team is not enough for some players. Some want to achieve personal glory; others may want to secure a permanent position on the team, to impress a new coach or a scout, or to atone for a poor performance in the past. Usually, such exaggerated ambitions have the opposite effect. The motto should be "Keep it simple; do what is possible; avoid foolish risks."

The Immediate Opponent

A quick, highly competitive opponent has to be handled with different technical and tactical methods than an opponent whose primary skills are technical. The latter is usually sensitive and less aggressive in one-on-one confrontations. In addition, his passes may not be very fast.

Many players use very distinct techniques and tactics; for instance, they use particular faking methods, or they have only one strong leg. A player should adjust his tactics accordingly during a game. Of course, it is an advantage to know these things about an opponent ahead of time.

The offensive player can also adjust to the particular style of a defensive player. The direct double pass is a good tactic to use against a defender who uses tight coverage during ball reception.

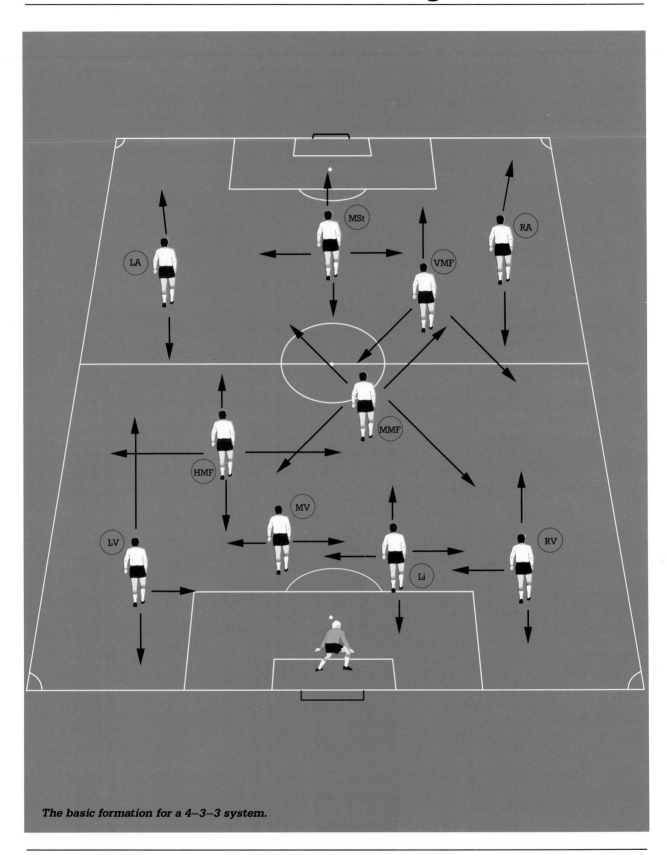

The basic formation for a 4–3–3 system.

Tactics and Tactical Training

System of Play

A system of play is the framework for tactical plans and actions. It can, however, also be part of the tactics themselves; for instance, when, for tactical reasons, a change in a particular game system is planned, or takes place.

> A system of play is the basic format that assigns distinct spaces on the playing field to each player for offensive and defensive movements and defines the tasks connected with those positions.

Teams that play modern soccer usually are not too closely tied to these spaces; as a matter of fact, in some circumstances players are even required to switch into spaces not assigned to them. It is important to note that switching spaces does not alter the basic system originally chosen. A change to another system occurs only when a player takes over the position of another player.

Characteristics of Modern Systems

Modern systems should have the following characteristics:

The drawings on pages 136, 138, 139, 141, and 142 show the basic positions and the spaces preferred for offensive and defensive actions in the systems played most commonly today.

The systems are: the 4–3–3 system (page 136); the 4–4–2 system (pages 138 and 139); the 3–5–2 system (page 141); and the 4–5–1 system (page 142).

- Players divided evenly over the field of play.
- Evenly divided responsibilities for each player.
- Strong defense of the goal.
- The ability to have the greatest possible number of players in the vicinity of the ball.
- The ability to change quickly from offense to defense.
- The participation of every player in offensive and defensive tasks.
- The ability to switch positions and tasks across the width and length of the field.
- Room for different opinions about the game and variations of group tactics.

Which system makes the most sense depends on the tactics chosen for a game, which players are available on a given day, how well different types of players work together, and the physical condition of each player.

Special Characteristics of the Individual Systems

The 4–3–3 System
In the 4–3–3 system, players are spread out over the field in a very balanced way. In this sense, it is similar to the W–M formation, which is not used anymore. This system has advantages for teams that do not have a great deal of tactical experience. It is, therefore, well suited for teams with young players.

In contrast to the systems we will discuss next, the 4–3–3 system has three forward positions. This has advantages and disadvantages. The advantage is that both wing positions are in place; this makes it easier for teams with less experience in tactics to play the wing and to switch sides.

However, by establishing definite positions for three forwards, the team loses some of the flexibility necessary to vary game tactics in midfield, where, for instance, the midfielders alternately move into the center forward position. Furthermore, it is easy for the opposition to see that the team is using the 4–3–3 system. And finally, the 4–3–3 system, with only three players in midfield, does not lend itself well to modern team and group tactics, such as space coverage and pressing.

The 4–4–2 System
In the 4–4–2 system, the midfield has been strengthened by one more player. This basic formation is more defensively oriented than the 4–3–3 system with its three forward positions.

The formation of the four midfielders can take the shape of a rectangle lying on its side or standing on one of its corners. The midfield player in front is expected to be the attacker in the open spaces on the left and right side of the center forward.

This system is particularly suited for teams with good tactical skills and players who are able to switch back and forth between midfield and forward positions. The considerable distances they have to cover, however, require exceptional endurance and speed.

Both forwards can function as outside and middle forward, or they can serve as a double point in front of the opponent's goal. In the latter case, the two wing positions are not covered, so that there is space for quick counterattacks by the defense from those positions or from the space in midfield to the sides.

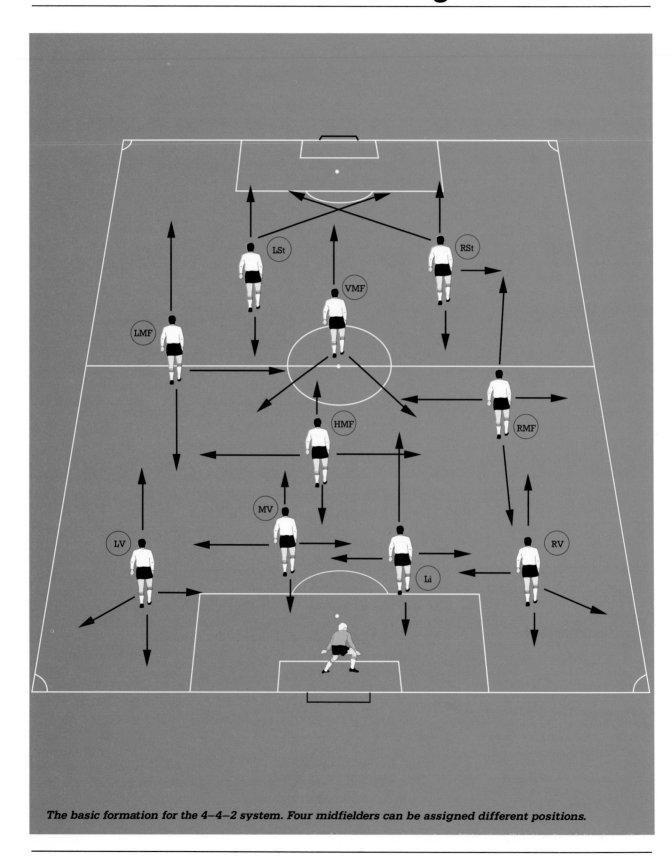

The basic formation for the 4—4—2 system. Four midfielders can be assigned different positions.

Three entirely different ways of organizing the positions of the four midfielders in the 4–4–2 system.

Tactics and Tactical Training

The positions of the midfielders are shown in the drawing on page 138.

The 3–5–2 System

This system evolved from the 4–4–2 system. Since almost every team today operates with only two center forward players, the last defensive barrier (with four defensive players) was "overstaffed." Two well-trained defensive players are perfectly capable of covering the two opposing center forwards one-on-one, if a free player (the sweeper) is safeguarding the open space in the rear.

Because of the tight, five-player formation in midfield, it is possible to use space coverage to safeguard the areas left and right of the centrally positioned defender's position. The large number of players in midfield makes it possible to use today's modern team tactics, such as fore-checking and pressing, ensuring a livelier and more attractive game.

The 4–5–1 System

The 4–5–1 system is a variation of the 3–5–2 system, which becomes an extreme form when the number of defensive players (at the expense of the center forward) is raised from three to four.

This system is used when teams need to reinforce the defense of the goal because they are playing a much stronger opponent. However, one of the basic demands of the modern systems of play—that players are to be divided evenly over the field—is not met. The biggest burden falls on the forward, since he is totally on his own. Two or three defenders are covering him, and he is seldom available to field a pass.

The double-video system (developed by Waldemar Winkler and Sony) can give important insights into a team's system. It can focus on the sequence of movements and the running route of every player.

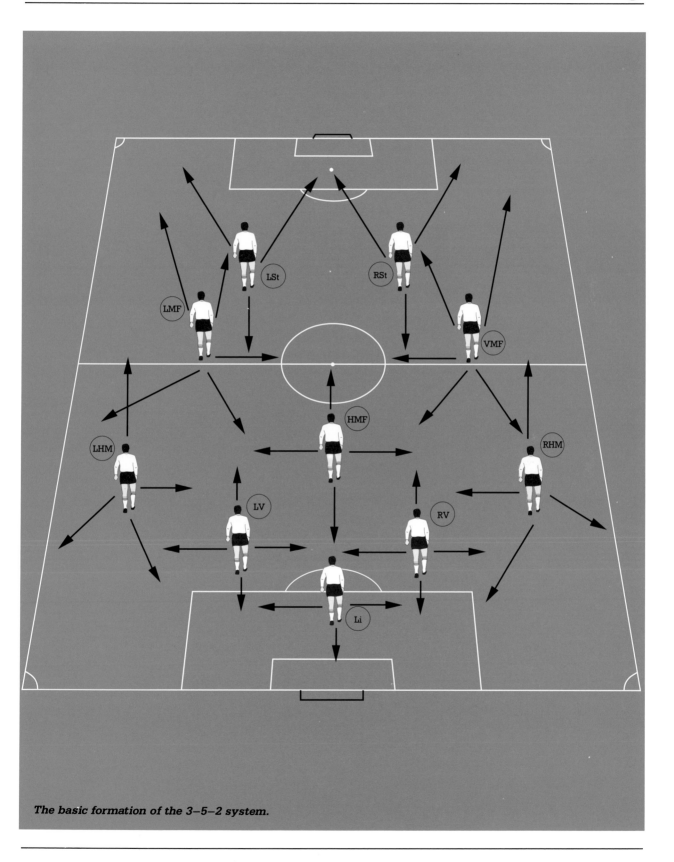

The basic formation of the 3—5—2 system.

Tactics and Tactical Training

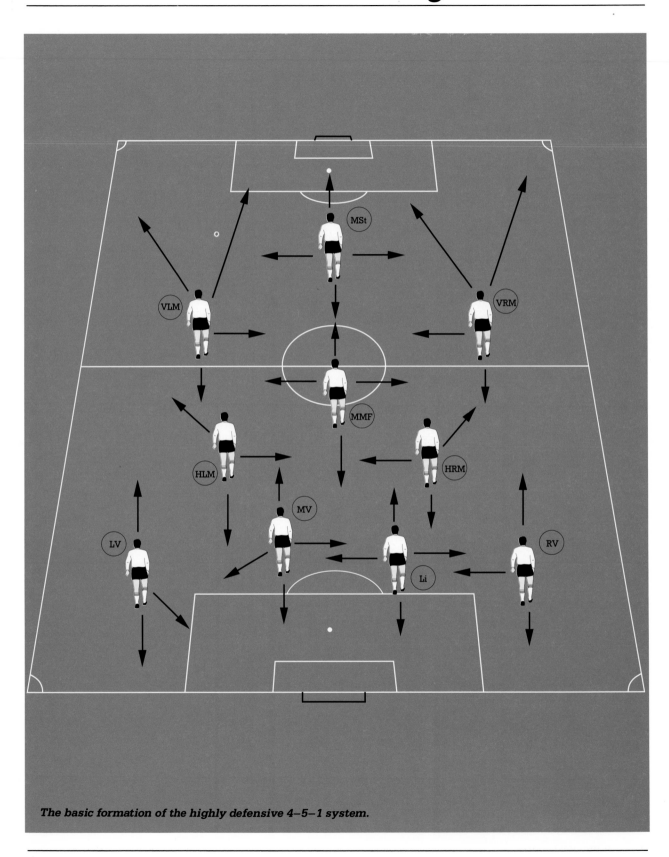

The basic formation of the highly defensive 4—5—1 system.

Style

Different teams develop totally different styles, depending on a club's tradition, the coach's philosophy, and the players.

> The special way that a team plays is shaped by the personality of the players and the coach and is known as its style.

Even before the turn of the century, many teams were known for their particular style of play. We still talk about:

- The English kick-and-rush style.
- The Scottish low-pass style.
- Schalker-Kreisel (circle/rotary style of the German club Schalcke).
- Czechoslovakian alley-way style.
- Austrian slicing style.

Top national and international teams distinguish themselves by the style of soccer they play. Many *South American* teams, notably those from Brazil, are characterized by their short passes. Their style is rich in techniques and full of tricks. The ball is moved around a great deal. Instead of moving the ball towards the opponent's goal the shortest possible way, the ball is passed back and forth, diagonally and across, in what becomes one long relay pass. The players satisfy their playfulness and show their technical skills at the same time. Suddenly, the game explodes with a through pass deep into enemy territory.

For years now, the *Belgian* and *Dutch national teams* have operated with forced fore-checking and cleverly designed offside traps. The opponent in possession of the ball is aggressively attacked in his own territory. Pressure is often applied by two, or even three, players. In order to prevent the opponents from launching a counterattack behind the back of the forward-moving team, the defenders arrange an aggressive offside trap.

Ever since the world championship games in 1982, the *Russian national team* has demonstrated an exceedingly fast game, often using direct passes across wide spaces. Almost every player moves with the attack and then retreats when the opposing team is on the offensive.

British teams still have a highly aggressive soccer style. Toughness and aggressiveness in one-on-one confrontations dominate. The tempo remains high throughout the game, or as long as the players' energy lasts. Tempo and rhythm changes, used effectively by other national teams, are rare for British teams.

Equipment and Accessories

Training Equipment

To "play" soccer, you only need a piece of grass and a ball. Presumably, this minimum need for equipment is one of the reasons why soccer is played all over the world. Lack of equipment never interferes with the fun of the game.

It is possible for teams to train with only a minimum of equipment. However, when a training program is oriented towards high performance with very differentiated skills, modern equipment should be available. A team that is well equipped can have a varied exercise program, permitting better training. In addition, the number of different exercises makes the training less monotonous and more fun.

Large Equipment

- Shooting walls (permanent and movable, with and without target markings) to improve kicking, passing, and driving skills (see photo).
- Ball suspended from an overhead structure.
- Suspended "Walker" ball (see photo, page 146).

Suspension balls are good for practising heading techniques, and for improving jumping strength in complex situations. Most of all, they are perfect for players practising on their own. The "Walker" model is best for simulating the motion of a ball in flight.

- Movable goals in different sizes.

By varying the number, position, and size of the goals, it is possible to use small game plays in many different ways and to adjust the training goals according to a given performance level for each player.

Small Equipment

- Soccer balls that are appropriate for different surfaces.

Most soccer balls have the same size and weight, but the material and color make them look different. For indoor soccer practice, it is best to use balls made of unlaminated leather or velour. Balls used on grass and on hard surfaces are also made from leather; however, the surface of the balls has been laminated to give them different degrees of resistance. For women and young players, lighter and smaller balls (for instance, size four instead of five) are recommended.

- Medicine balls.

Medicine balls come in different weights and sizes. They are particularly suited for special conditioning training. They allow players to engage in endurance and strength training playfully.

- Identification shirts.

Most of the neon-colored shirts are light, perspiration-repellent, quick to dry, and hygienic. They are big, well-fitting, and can easily be worn over a sweat suit. These shirts are very helpful in identifying different training groups.

- Identification poles and cones.

Well-planned training sessions constantly change zones, goals, and locations. Plastic marking poles are useful for almost every type of ground condition.

- Hurdles.

Easy to transport and quickly adjustable for height, hurdles are a valuable aid in developing jumping strength. They are also very helpful for fitness training (hurdle races and relay races).

- Practice "dummies."

These are life-size figures made out of wood or plastic that can be carried or wheeled around. They are helpful for practising corner kicks and free kicks. A player can practise these skills by himself.

- Power equipment and dumbbells.

The equipment for general power training is too expensive for most teams. It is available in modern fitness gyms that provide qualified instructors. Sometimes, it is possible to contract with them to allow use by the players. Power equipment is recommended for rehabilitation training after injuries.

For specific power training, a club should invest in small equipment. The following equipment has proved to be effective:

- Weights.
- Ankle weights.
- Weighted shoes.
- Sandbags.
- Jumping ropes.

With these aids a coach can put together a power-training program that is both effective and fun for the players.

Equipment and Accessories

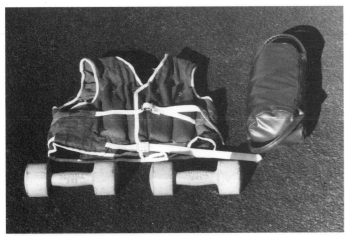
Sandbag, weighted vest, short dumbbells.

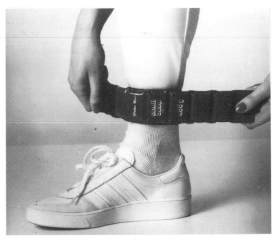
Ankle weight.

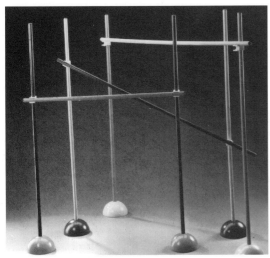
Adjustable hurdles for a variety of uses.

Balls of all types are needed for training.

The "dummy" as a passive opponent. Suspended ball, the Walker model.

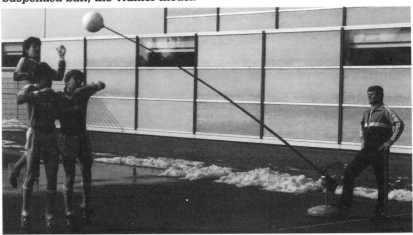

Equipment and Accessories

Markings and slalom poles have many different uses.

Goals of different sizes can also be used for shooting with targets.

Rollers on the goal box make it movable.

Equipment and Accessories

Accessories

In addition to the training equipment discussed above, coaches and players need personal accessories for training and competition.

Accessories for the Player

- Short, tricot, woollen gaiters.
- Sweat suit.
- Studded shoes and tools.
- Cleats.
- Shoes for play on hard ground and indoors.
- Shin guards.
- Athletic supporter.
- Elastic bandages and tapes.
- Arm band for the captain of the team.
- Goalkeeper's cap.
- Bag for personal gear.

Clothing worn for training and competition is usually supplied by the team. Obviously, the material should be adapted to the climate. Tricots are a good choice because of the combination of man-made fibres and old-fashioned cotton and wool. The outside of the material draws perspiration away, preventing the player from catching a cold. On particularly cold days, the player can protect himself with additional underwear (tights). The color of the clothing should be chosen carefully. It should stand out against the opponent's uniforms and the background. Green tricots and shorts are as bad when playing on grass as is dark clothing when playing under the lights. Wild-patterned clothing is not suitable for the same reason.

Soccer shoes—just in case:

High-tops for the winter.

Normal shoes with removable cleats.

Multi-cleated rubber soles.

Normal rubber-cleated soles.

Comfortable, functional training suit.

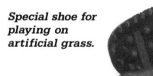

Special shoe for playing on artificial grass.

Special shoe for playing indoors.

Each player should choose his own soccer shoes. Of course, a coach can give professional advice.

Today, shoes with short rubber or plastic cleats are used almost exclusively because they put much less stress on the ankle and knee joints. With the new arrangement of these cleats, the same shoes can also be worn for competition. Children and young players should not wear anything else for competition or for training.

Senior players, however, do still use deeply cleated shoes for extra-secure gripping when playing in long grass and in snow. Expensive shoes have ceramic material added to the cleats for better traction. These shoes are strongly recommended for hard surfaces, artificial surfaces, and most of all for indoors. Normal soccer shoes are not well suited for these types of surfaces. Quick changes in direction are difficult and can permanently damage the ankle and knee joints.

Many accessories are available to protect against injuries. Knee and shin protection are mandatory for many professional players. What is good for professionals is also good for young and amateur players. An athletic supporter provides effective protection and is strongly recommended. Elastic bandages and tapes offer good support after injuries. And last, but not least, a well-equipped bag with items for personal hygiene is a must for every player.

Equipment and Accessories

Accessories for the Coach

- Whistle.
- Tactical game board (see below).
- Training log.
- Tape recorder.
- First-aid kit.
- Thermos bottle for ice water.
- Supply of cleats.

The coach must be well equipped for the varied tasks of training and competition. More than coaching responsibilities await the coach of young and amateur teams. Often he is masseur, counselor, and "medicine man" of the team—and often all at the same time.

For most coaches, the referee's whistle is standard equipment. However, some coaches have stopped using a whistle. They feel that commands become too militaristic when using a whistle.

Very few coaches have a tactical game board, a training log, or a tape recorder. The tactical board (now available in a relatively small format that can be folded) is a very useful training tool. Before a game, it can be used to demonstrate important tactical choices; during a game (at halftime) it is useful for conveying information in a visual form. The training log is a perfect place to record important data from training sessions and from competition. Over time, this data becomes a valuable aid in long-term planning. It also helps to control and evaluate all training and game decisions. The tape recorder (one that fits in the palm of the hand) allows the coach to record important observations during the game. Unrecorded observations tend to get lost during the excitement of the game.

If a coach is also the "medicine man," he will want to have a first-aid kit on hand, as well as a supply of cleats.

A thermos bottle filled with ice and water is strongly recommended for first-aid after injuries, such as bruises and pulled ligaments or muscles. The immediate application of ice greatly reduces the amount of bleeding into the tissue. This, in turn, reduces healing time. Ice spray, which was used for a long time, does not have nearly the same effect as ice water, because it only affects the surface.

The tactical game board is a very valuable tool for the coach. He can demonstrate objectives and tasks before a training session or a game. He can also illustrate mistakes.

Preparation for Competition

In everyday language, training is also defined as preparation for competition. In that sense, training is extremely important. It is a process that, for some players, stretches over many years and sometimes even decades. In addition, however, every player must think in terms of short-term goals and use training as a preparation for every competition. The following aspects are important when preparing for any competition:

• Proper nutrition.
• Motivation.
• Mental attitude.
• Warming up.
• Cooling down.

Nutrition

For athletes, proper nutrition means eating properly before, during, and after competition. Sadly, most people know very little about what constitutes proper nutrition. In fact, the human organism is really not very different from an engine. A sophisticated engine needs superior fuel and oil in order to function properly.

This is also true for a player. The higher the demand for a superior performance, in training and in competition, the higher the nutritional value must be.

Proper nutrition requires sufficient amounts of the following:

• Nutritional value.
• Essential minerals.
• Vitamins.
• Liquids.

At the yearly conference of the Association of German Soccer Teachers (1989), Max Inzinger, the nutritional counselor for the FIFA, outlined the basic requirements for proper nutrition. What follow are Inzinger's recommendations.

Nutrition that is deficient in essential elements can have dire physiological and psychological consequences for an athlete, such as:

• Lack of concentration.
• General tiredness.
• Little energy.
• Muscle cramps.
• Blackouts.
• Visual problems.
• Shortness of breath.

What follow are the basic requirements for proper nutrition and liquid intake:

• Proper caloric intake must be established individually for every player.
• Carbohydrate storage must be sufficient.
• Increased demand for vitamins must be taken into account.
• Availability of electrolytes and minerals must be assured.
• Body fluids must be balanced through proper fluid intake.

Individual Caloric Needs

The amount of energy an individual needs depends on the person's constitution, the amount of daily pressure, and the frequency of his or her training. According to Inzinger, the daily caloric intake is calculated with the following formula:

Body size × a value number = energy needs

A player who is six feet (180 cm) tall and is training between one and two hours (not counting any other activities) needs a daily caloric intake of 3960 calories. The individual value number is calculated according to the following table:

Value number	Training frequency
18	1–2 times weekly
20	3–4 times weekly
22	1–2 hours daily
24	3–4 hours daily
28	5–6 hours daily

Proper Eating Habits

The old saying "A student with a full belly can't study" holds true for an athlete. According to the findings of nutritional scientists, there are several reasons why it is better to change from eating a few large meals to eating frequent small meals.

Inzinger recommends the following meal schedule:

7:00 AM:	Breakfast 20 percent of the daily calories
9:00 AM:	First snack 10 percent of the daily calories
10:30 AM:	Second snack 5 percent of the daily calories
12:00 noon:	Lunch 20 percent of the daily calories
2:00 PM:	Third snack 10 percent of the daily calories
5:00 PM:	Fourth snack 5 percent of the daily calories
7:00 PM:	Dinner 20 percent of the daily calories
9:00 PM:	Late snack 10 percent of the daily calories

Preparation for Competition

Nutrition Rich in Carbohydrates

Ideally, every meal should consist mainly of those foods that are needed before and after different kinds of activities. For intellectually active people, protein is essential; for physically active people, and especially for athletes, carbohydrates are vital.

The total nutritional needs for a soccer player involved in competition and training can be broken down as follows:

- Carbohydrates   60 percent
- Fat   25 percent
- Protein   15 percent

In general, a player should consume one ounce of carbohydrates for every eight pounds (7 g for every kg) of body weight.

The amount of protein needs to be increased whenever a training schedule is heavy and after an injury. In order for the body to have the optimum amount of carbohydrates available at the time of a match, some nutritional scientists recommend a "carbohydrate binge":

- Two days before a game, eat food low in carbohydrates.
- The day before and the day of a game, eat carbohydrate-rich foods.

By reducing the intake of carbohydrates two days before a game, the body goes into carbohydrate deficit. The body adjusts by creating a kind of hypercompensation reaction.

Carbohydrates are found in many different foods. The time it takes to convert carbohydrates (sugar metabolism) to energy differs for specific athletic performances and depends on the type of food consumed. For example:

- Whole-wheat bread   60–240 minutes
- Fruits and vegetables   60–100 minutes
- Bread and baked goods   40–60 minutes
- Sweets and sweet drinks   15–40 minutes
- Glucose   10–20 minutes

It makes sense to adjust a player's food intake so that he will have a large supply of carbohydrates at the appropriate time. Approximately two hours before the game, the player should eat whole-wheat products. Later, small amounts of dry, baked goods should be consumed. Later still, the player needs something sweet to drink.

Importance of Vitamins

Vitamins are the catalysts that create energy through metabolism. According to Inzinger, an athlete's need for vitamins is three to four times as high as it is for normally active people. The following vitamins are of special importance:

- Vitamins A, B_1, B_2, B_6, and B_{12}.
- Vitamin C.
- Vitamin D.

High amounts of these vitamins can be found in:

- Whole-wheat products.
- Potatoes.
- Brown rice.
- Fresh fruit.
- Fresh vegetables.

White bread, white rice, and cooked fruits and vegetables have a much lower vitamin content.

Essential Minerals

Of the numerous minerals essential to the human body, the following are of particular importance for the athlete:

- Potassium.
- Sodium.
- Calcium.
- Magnesium.
- Iron.
- Iodine.

According to Max Inzinger, two-thirds of all athletes suffer from magnesium deficiency. Normal nutrition needs to be supplemented with magnesium. This is particularly important because our food contains only very small amounts of this essential mineral. During times of intense athletic activities, it is recommended that players also take potassium, iron, and iodine supplements.

Replacing Body Fluids

In the course of a hard-fought competition in high temperatures, a player can lose up to three quarts (3 l) of fluids. This loss must be corrected quickly. Because essential minerals are also lost during times of increased perspiration, water alone is not sufficient.

It is essential to replace fluids and electrolytes during the game (at halftime), as well as after the game. It is important to use the proper fluids and to give them at the right time.

Proper Fluids

Proper fluids are those with the appropriate amounts of sugar and essential minerals. Very sweet fruit juices and sodas with a high sugar content are generally not recommended. Instead, use mineral water with a low sodium content and a high magnesium content.

Isotonic drinks may be used if the sodium content is low and the content of calcium, potassium, and magnesium is high.

Whenever players prepare their own drinks from mineral powder, they must follow the directions carefully. High doses of electrolytes can cause counterreactions and increased water loss. Players can mix themselves a very good drink by combining fruit juices, tea, and mineral water.

Proper Intake of Liquids

The way the drink is taken is as important as the type of drink used:

- Immediately before, during, and after the game, it is essential that drinks be taken in small sips, not gulped. However, a large amount of liquids can be taken two hours before and after the game.
- Thirst should be quenched with warm or lukewarm drinks rather than very cold drinks. Cold drinks inhibit hunger because they remain in the stomach longer than warmer liquids. The result is that a player will not eat the quantity of food he needs after the stress of the game.
- Finally, there is nothing wrong with a glass of beer after the game. This can be taken with, or better yet, after a meal.

Motivation

The impact of motivation on the level of performance has already been mentioned in the chapter on tactical skills. A player who is overly motivated will be nervous and uptight. However, he can also be under-motivated, which will lead to a poor performance, listless play, and a lack of interest. Neither of these levels of motivation are conducive to good, competitive performances. In general, we distinguish between:

- Self-motivation.
- Motivation from the outside (the coach, teammates, friends, etc.).

How motivation influences performance becomes clear when we look at the process of motivation.

The Motivational Process

Human beings are motivated to action (and to athletic performances) for many different reasons:

- Need to move.
- Need to play.
- Need for recognition.

For human beings, motivation as an impulse usually develops over time through education and other external influences. One legitimate motivation in professional sports is the expectation of financial rewards. Another, less effective factor is fear, which, sadly, often plays a large role. Fear can keep a player from attempting risky tackles and from diving for passes.

Many conflicting motives and needs influence a player's level of motivation. Sometimes, motives and needs are not apparent until external situations and conditions are favorable. A player may be unaware of some of his motives, or

he may not know the reasons for them and needs to do some work in order to understand them. At times, the coach or teammates may have to assist him with this.

For instance, a coach might have to curb a new player's overly aggressive actions on the field. The new player might be trying to win a permanent position on the team. During the same game, it might be necessary for the coach to push an older player, who has been with the team for a long time and has lost some of his motivation.

Accordingly, the process of motivation can be defined as follows:

> A player's motives and needs as incentives for action are activated, made conscious, actualized, and guided to bring them into harmony with the demands of a given day.

Performance-enhancing Motives and Needs

The following are motives and needs that can positively influence the level of performance in sports:

Motives

- Ambition.
- Outside recognition.
- Love of performing in front of an audience.
- Social standing.
- Sociability.
- Lack of self-confidence.
- Love of travel.

Preparation for Competition

Needs

- To be active and moving.
- To expend excess energy.
- To obtain self-fulfillment.
- To dissipate aggressive tendencies.
- To enjoy the play instinct.
- To be active.
- To take risks.
- To use the hunting instinct.
- To satisfy curiosity.
- To take advantage of the adventure instinct.

Overall, motives and needs are guided by two basic factors:

- The hope of success.
- The fear of failure.

Experience has shown that soccer players are more motivated by their hope for success than by their fear of failure. The anticipation of a win, the celebration that usually follows, and the possibility of the team moving up in the standings should be emphasized in motivating players, rather than the consequences of failure.

Setting Attractive Goals

The effect of motivation on players depends to a great degree on how attractive the goal is. It is not easy to motivate players when the only result of winning a game is that the team moves one point closer to the team ahead of them. A significant jump in the standings, however, would make a great deal of difference in the level of motivation. Furthermore, a coach can influence his players by his own attitude and in the way he values the outcome of the team's efforts. If necessary, the coach has to adjust his presentation of the goal in order to maximize the motivation of individual players and the team.

For instance, to reach the desired goal he might say, "A tie is OK"; or, "Only a big win can be considered a success"; or, "Let's treat the fans to a beautiful game."

Interim Stages of Motivation

An essential aspect of motivation is the chance players have of achieving a desired goal. But objectives that seem to be too easy or too difficult to accomplish are approached with overconfidence and carelessness or with hesitancy and too little confidence. Experience has shown that dividing a goal into several subgoals works well.

It is the responsibility of the coach to state a goal in such a way that the players are convinced (without becoming arrogant) that they have a chance to be successful. In his efforts to define a particular subgoal, the coach must be careful not to lose credibility. Players are sensitive and well able to detect oversimplification and exaggeration. Motivation using either of these tactics falls on deaf ears. Clearly, it is difficult to properly motivate a team. All attempts must take into consideration each player's individual level of motivation and the actual demands that are being made on the player and the team as a whole.

Mental Training

In the beginning, we talked about the importance of self-motivation as a stimulus for a player's performance.

Mental training is important for self-motivation. Visualization training can be very helpful. For this kind of training, a player must relax himself psychologically and physically. This relaxed state allows him to be receptive to self-generated or outside affirmations ("You *are* successful") and to visual images (seeing himself dribbling successfully or going through the motions of a perfect combination play). We know, for instance, that Paul Breitner uses this technique in order to prepare himself mentally for an important game. The necessary state of relaxation can only be achieved in a calm and quiet atmosphere. In such a state, a player is able to:

- Run through technical and tactical tasks.
- Devise special strategies for handling a particular opponent.
- Reduce imagined fears.
- Develop self-confidence through self-hypnosis.

Surely, mental training is not for every player, and not only because life in the locker room is so hectic. Most players are not open to such sensitive techniques.

They lack the knowledge and the ability to reach the necessary state of relaxation. For those players who are interested, and for those who find it difficult to prepare themselves for a game for psychological reasons, mental training is highly recommended. The coach may want to seek the advice of a sports psychologist.

Preparation for Competition

Overcoming Pre-game Stress

Soccer has its share of "World Champion Training" teams that fall apart under the pressure of competition. But aside from those exceptions, many experienced players suffer from pre-game stress before important games. Their feelings are usually caused by fears of failure and are hard to put into words. Occasionally, a player has very concrete worries, such as fearing an opponent who is well known for his toughness, or concerns about reinjuring himself. Other stress is often caused by an exaggerated expectation on the part of the fans, created by the media. Many other factors can contribute to the level of stress, such as a strange environment, ecstatic fans, extreme weather conditions, etc.

The effects of stress are as different as they are numerous. They range from physiological changes that can be measured objectively, such as changes in pulse rate, changes in reaction time, and increased muscle tone, to psychological effects, such as changes in personal habits. It is common to see an increase in the level of adrenaline during periods of stress. Although adrenaline is necessary for high levels of physical performance, it will actually decrease the level of performance if the body releases too much of it.

What can a coach and a player do to maintain the proper level of adrenaline? Psychologists recommend special relaxation methods, such as autogenous training, progressive muscle relaxation, and biofeedback. However, for soccer, these methods have not been very effective.

The following methods have been more successful:
- Providing players with objective information about the opposing team and their specific opponent.
- Giving each player clear and precise instructions about the tactical tasks he is responsible for.
- Explaining the risks a player is expected to take and informing him about what support he can expect.
- Creating a realistic understanding of the demands that might have been distorted by outside influences.
- Appealing to team work ("One for all, all for one").
- Assigning the tasks that lie ahead for every player.
- Decreasing fears an individual player might have.
- Providing time for extensive warm-up training.

Warm-up and Cool Down

The warm-up takes place immediately before a game; cooling down, immediately after a game. Both measures are of vital importance for activating high levels of performance. Several different methods for warming up are available:
- Mental warm-ups (see above).
- Passive warm-ups (i.e., with warm bath and massage).
- Active warm-ups for the body.
  We will discuss only the last aspect of the warm-up.

Importance of Warm-up Training

Before starting to train or exercise, and before every game, a player should go through a purposeful, systematic warm-up. The importance of this has been widely acknowledged. A warm-up is the best prevention against injuries, and it maximizes the effect and success of training, as well as performance during a game. Sad to say, this is still not taken seriously enough by many players. All too often, the result is a micro-injury consisting of small tears in the muscle fibres. Over the span of weeks and months, these small injuries add up to serious muscle damage.

A systematic warm-up program that slowly increases in intensity will warm up the muscles by about four degrees (two degrees C) and increase flexibility by 20 percent. Thus, a proper warm-up considerably reduces the chances of injury and speeds up reaction times. In competition, a player must be ready to produce 100 percent in terms of energy and speed during the first few minutes, so a proper warm-up is essential.

Furthermore, the protective mechanism of the muscle system is usually reduced due to stress. Here, too, a warm-up period is beneficial.

In addition to these well-known, injury-preventing factors, a systematic warm-up before a game has other positive effects:

- The circulatory system slowly and safely prepares the organism for the increase in the physical stress load that lies ahead. This process is similar to warming up the engine before taking a car on the road.

Preparation for Competition

- Metabolic processes essential for high levels of activities are slowly primed, making energy available through metabolism, delaying the letdown, and saving important carbohydrate reserves for the extra energy required at the end of a game.
- Excess adrenaline is reduced, which in turn reduces pre-game jitters (see above).
- Tight muscles (from a previous training session or following a long trip to the stadium) can be relieved through proper stretching exercises.
- Work with the ball increases ball-handling and soccer-specific techniques. This is especially important for young and amateur players, who usually only train twice a week. Every player knows the importance of the first pass in a game. Good ball handling, therefore, is particularly important in the first few minutes of a game.
- During the warm-up, a player has a chance to get to know the field of play. That is immeasurably important in "away" games. Players get a feeling for the new field or stadium and its very specific atmosphere.
- Last, but not least, soccer is a team sport and warm-up training supports the player's sense of belonging to the social structure of the team.

Structure of Warm-up Training

Depending on the age, level of training, and outside temperature, a warm-up period should last at least 15 to 30 minutes. The better the level of training, the older the player, and the lower the temperature, the longer the warm-up should be. It is clear that systematic warm-up training before a game should not be suspended, even when the outside temperature is high.

Warm-up training can be programmed according to the following basic guidelines:
- Five to ten minutes' slow jogging.
- Five to ten minutes' passive stretching.
- Five minutes' work with the ball, going over all the important techniques.
- Two minutes of 100-foot (30-m) runs, steadily increasing in speed until the maximum level is reached.
- Five minutes' work with the ball, practising position-specific techniques.
- Approximately 10 short sprints, stops, and changes of direction, all with maximum speed.

After the warm-up, every player should show visible signs of perspiration. Often players will change their shirt before going on the field. This is a good time for the coach to say a few encouraging words.

Importance of Cool Down

It was West Germany's Sepp Herberger who said, "After the game equals before the game." In other words, what is proper to do before a game is also proper after a game. Although he was referring to the inner, mental attitude of the players, this idea is valid for the physical aspects of the game. Contrary to former times, every player has an additional task after the game: to cool down.

Track and field athletes, whose success depends entirely on their own, personal fitness and not on the performance of teammates, have long understood the importance of cooling down. For these athletes, the warm-up and the cool down usually take much longer than the actual competition. Many soccer teams now also understand the need for a good cool-down period. They do not wait until the next day. Instead, they include a 15-minute cool-down period in their overall program. This might involve warm baths, massages, and an actual recuperation program.

The same basic system is important for young players and amateur teams. They should schedule a cool-down period after every game, particularly during a championship series. Players who have a cool-down period will be in much better shape for the next game than will any opponents who do not.

What is the rationale, and what are the positive effects, of such a cool down? What form should it take? Uric-acid measurements have shown that the level of fatigue the day after a game is much lower for a player who has undergone a cool-down period after a game. This exercise increases the amount of uric acid released by the body. Uric acid is a by-product of metabolism, accumulating in the body as a result of physical activity. It is a sign of the body's level of fatigue and of the time needed for recuperation.

Metric Conversion

Structure of a Cool-down Program
- Time   At least 10 to 15 minutes
- Tempo   Slow jog
- Pulse rate   Approximately 130 beats per minute

Additionally, a warm bath and massage can be helpful. Running should be followed by loosening and stretching exercises.

Closing Wishes from the Author

The discussion of the cooling-down concept has brought us full circle. After studying the information contained between the covers of this book, it is up to you to transfer all your newfound knowledge to your daily training sessions.

I hope you have great fun, but more than that, even greater success!

Yours!
Gerhard Bauer

Metric Conversion

Note: Within the text and diagrams, approximate equivalencies only are used, except where regulation measurements are involved. Values are generally rounded to be useful when yards and feet are most familiar or when metres are preferred by the coach.

Feet	Yards	Metres	Feet	Yards	Metres
1	⅓	0.305	24	8	7.32
2	⅔	0.610	25	8⅓	7.63
3	1	0.914	27	9	8.23
6	2	1.83	30	10	9.14
9	3	2.74	45	15	13.73
10	3⅓	3.05	60	20	18.3
12	4	3.66	90	30	27.45
15	5	4.57	120	40	36.6
18	6	5.49	150	50	45.7
20	6⅔	6.10	230	77	70
21	7	6.40	344	115	105

Index

Index